Travels with
Abraham
and
Sarah

Travels with
Abraham
and
Sarah

IN SEARCH OF A GODLY MARRIAGE

Lyndon Akins

WinePressPublishing
Great Books, Defined.

WinePress Publishing (PO Box 428, Enumclaw, WA 98022) functions only as book publisher. As such, the ultimate design, content, editorial accuracy, and views expressed or implied in this work are those of the author.

ISBN 13: 978-1-4141-2036-2
ISBN 10: 1-4141-2036-2
Library of Congress Catalog Card Number: 2011921672

This book is dedicated to my wife, Terry, for her encouragement, love, and support, and to my professors at Luther Rice Seminary. May God be praised and glorified through this book.

Contents

Foreword

"A TRIP, A safari, an exploration, is an entity, different from all other journeys...In this a journey is like a marriage. It has a personality, temperament, individuality, uniqueness...The certain way to be wrong is to think you control it" (John Steinbeck, *Travels with Charlie: In Search of America,* pg. 4). I first read that quote from John Steinbeck's book when I was a sophomore at The University of Tennessee. Even after many career years, marriage, fatherhood, and obtaining a Masters of Divinity degree from Luther Rice Seminary, Mr. Steinbeck's words and pace still draw me into his journey that was undertaken with a black poodle named Charlie.

Over the years, I have found that in many ways, marriage is a journey. My wife, Terry, and I lead a Sunday Bible study class at Dunwoody Baptist Church of newly married couples who are on the spiritual and emotional journey of marriage. I call them a group from "I do to goo." They join our class shortly after they marry (I do), and now babies are being born to those couples (babies say "goo"). At one point, those class members requested a study on marriage. Even though my seminary focus was not in marriage counseling, I took on the challenge to provide Bible based teaching that addresses God's plan for marriage. While there are many exceptional Christian resources, I found little in terms of books that looked at marriage from the vantage point of married Bible characters. That is when I recalled John Steinbeck's inspiring book on discovering the experiences and wisdom of the people who have made America a special place to call home. He did not simply research demographics or philosopher and historian's interpretations. Instead he bought a camper, loaded up his canine companion and began a physical journey to live among the people whose lives wove a patchwork quilt of the American lifestyle. I therefore asked God to help me write one based upon actual events in the life of a well-known couple from the Bible: Abraham and Sarah. The worldly events they encountered provide the framework for discussing their spiritual journey and how that journey led them into a deeper, more meaningful relationship with each other and God.

The story of Abraham and Sarah is about an ancient couple in a Near Eastern land, but contemporary Christian married couples should be able to identify with Abraham and Sarah's challenges, desires, and faith. They made a lot of mistakes, but they wisely turned to the God of grace and mercy. Godly people today make similar mistakes of the heart, and they hurt one another or innocent bystanders. However, if we are committed to God and one another through it all, then God will be glorified, we will be blessed, and others will be encouraged through our marriage examples.

In conclusion, I must disclose that this book is not intended to be a detailed exegesis of every verse covering the life of Abraham and Sarah. Instead it is a story rooted

Foreword

in Scripture for the serious Bible student desiring a strong and lasting relationship with their spouse and God. This book is intended to encourage you to read and enjoy God's Word, and to apply His practical and timeless truths for marriage. In my opening quote of John Steinbeck's book he states that a, "journey is like a marriage...and the certain way to be wrong is to think you control it." I invite you to take a spiritual journey through my book, and recognize that the biggest mistakes Abraham and Sarah made were the ones when they thought they controlled things. Only after learning to trust and follow God's Word did they arrive at their destination of a godly marriage.

I pray that this book and God's Word draw you into a journey with Abraham and Sarah. May you ponder God's truths, find applications in your life from the illustrations, grow old in love with your spouse, and always include God on your marriage journey.

—Lyndon (Lyn) R. Akins
2011

CHAPTER 1

• •

The Journey Map
(Genesis 12–22)

T HE STORY OF Abraham and Sarah (originally
Abram and Sarai) is one of adventure, faith, travel,
and the pursuit of a godly marriage. Although their
experiences occurred in an ancient era, their journey cap-
tures timeless truths that we can apply to our marriages today. Abraham and Sarah illustrate that successful marriages
don't just happen. Instead, they occur through the grace
of God and His relationship with each individual couple.

Statisticians tell us that 50% of marriages fail, but even
that grim number illustrates that the institution of marriage
is not a failure. People have a God-given desire for love, commitment, and marriage. Relationships continue to lead people
to the altar of matrimony. And even those getting divorced
often find they return to a new marriage relationship.

Yet God's desire for marriage is not that we keep
marrying and divorcing until we get things right. In fact,
the Bible states that God hates divorce (Malachi 2:16),
and Jesus stated that divorce was not God's intent for
marriage (Mark 10:2–9). God wants us to be intimately

involved in a long-term covenant relationship, but it isn't easy or automatic just because we are Christians. Godly marriages require an intentional pursuit of God's plan for relationships. That intentional pursuit is required of both husband and wife.

Regardless of how our pagan society and government officials view or try to regulate marriage, Christians have a firm biblical foundation that supports our adherence to the marriage covenant that God created. In fact, God will not hold us accountable for society's laws about marriage, divorce, and relationships. Instead, God holds each man accountable for his own decisions. Your choices may have negative consequences in a society possessing a "flip-flop morality," but God's truth is unchanging.

Christians need not stumble over the sin of the world and follow its confused moral compass. Christ stated that Satan is the prince of this world, and it is evident that he has plenty of willing accomplices who want to destroy marriages and families. Therefore Christians must look to God and His Word as it is recorded in the Bible for directions on how to have a marriage that will glorify Him. People like Dr. Phil and Oprah have sincere ideas on the subject of marriage, and some of their suggestions may work for the short term. But if you want eternal, long-term results, then you are better served by consulting the inventor of marriage: the Lord God!

Your marriage is a journey, but you and your spouse need not take this journey alone. Your Creator wants to accompany you on the adventure. His plans are to bless and prosper your marriage, and in turn, you will glorify Him by keeping the covenant He created. He will allow you flexibility during the journey as He is a God of free will, but the certain way to be wrong is to think you can be successful without Him.

Marriage was created as a two-party covenant involving three people: you and your spouse, living as one, and God. Godless marriages will work for a while, and not all will end in divorce, but without God, they are guaranteed to end in emptiness. Without God in your marriage, you have found something else to fill God's role. The Bible describes that situation as "idolatry."

Paul writes in 1 Timothy 2:5–6, "For there is one God and one mediator between God and men, the man Christ Jesus…" In many cases, the ancient people would create a visible carving or statue (an idol) and believe that it possessed the ability to provide for their happiness or wellbeing. But an idol doesn't need to be visual. Things like desires for wealth, power, attention, pleasure, or entertainment can consume our thoughts and become idols, and in turn, they will control our actions. Married couples cannot submit to godly living if they are spending all their energy on achieving success on the world's terms.

So, can people have successful, godly marriages and also enjoy success in the world? The best way I know to answer that question is to say that it is totally God's decision. I have seen some godly people who are very wealthy and equally godly couples who do not have two nickels to rub together. I believe that the world wants us to believe that life is a decision between feast and famine. However, a relationship with God requires that you trust and follow Christ's plan for your life and marriage and then allow Him to bless you as He desires.

Abraham followed God's words in faith, and God provided for his daily needs. This provision was then followed by God blessing Abraham beyond his needs. We often just do not desire or appreciate what God is offering! Everything we receive each day is a gift: breath, life, food, sunlight—and the list goes on. But we think of these things as "givens" or the basic elements that God is required to provide. Then we want what other people possess. We look at our lives and compare them to the neighbor and say, "Why can't I have what that family has instead?" We are not thankful for God's gifts and provision.

God had a gift planned for Abram and Sarai that they could not imagine. Having a baby at their advanced ages was as impossible then as it is today. That is why they tried pursuing a child through a surrogate mother. Abram and Sarai never had experienced a God of the impossible, or one who made and kept promises. They also possessed a bit of our modern personality, as they were unable to accept a gift.

Have you found this to be the case with family or friends? We have become a people unable to accept a gift because it might not be exactly what we want. Therefore we require gift cards, and retailers are making a fortune off of the concept. Do you have family or friends who are becoming impossible to please concerning gift giving? First of all, they have too much stuff already. Then there is the pressure of topping last year's gift, and that challenge only grows in expense and stress. Then there are people who do not really want a gift; they just want you to fulfill an order. "Just send me money," is what I am told. What an empty relationship! All the fun of giving is drained out of your wallet and into a colorful, plastic card.

Some people leave no room in their lives for a gift. They never experience the joy of giving and watching the moment of surprise or the joy of receiving what someone wants to give them. Unfortunately, many of us have this kind of relationship with God. We approach Him with an attitude of, "Just answer the prayer. And if you cannot do that, then give me a gift card, and I'll get it myself." Here is where we need to be careful in our daily attitudes. Ask yourself: if I am willing to treat family and friends in such an impersonal and demanding way, am I approaching God in the same way? If there is a hint of a "yes" answer in your mind, then you should be concerned that you are treating your spouse with the same attitude.

A marriage that is first and foremost focused on obtaining and attaining what the world offers will lead to a godless marriage. As a couple, you will lack the ability to have the fruitfulness that God's marriage covenant promises. The Bible tells us, "God blessed them [their marriage] and said to them, "Be fruitful and increase in number; fill the earth and subdue it. Rule [manage] over the fish of the sea and the birds of the air, and over every living creature that moves on the ground." Then God saw all that He had made, and it was very was good..." (selection from Gen. 1:28–31). God created the perfect scenario in marriage. Therefore it cannot be experienced apart from Him. God first wants a couple to approach Him as one flesh and mind and to have an obedient relationship with Him. In turn, He will bless the couple's life on earth (and into eternity) beyond their best daydream! Just remember that everything and everyday is a gift.

Before we evaluate Abram and Sari's marriage and their faith journey, let's review the benchmarks of God's initial plan for marriage as it is outlined in the Bible. Please take a moment and read these Scripture selections: Gen. 1:26–31 and 2:18–25.

After reading those passages, we can begin to see how God's grace is reflected in His creation, which is an indication of how He wants us to live with and relate to one another. God's mercy and grace are a roadmap for marriage. And just as God was merciful and gracious with Adam and Eve in light of their disobedience, we, too, are to treat our husband or wife with mercy and grace.

God has shed His grace and mercy upon man since the beginning; yet, there were earthly consequences to sinful actions. Does that concept sound unfair to you? Some people imagine God as a permissive grandfather who overlooks our lifestyle choices with a wink and a nod. Others describe Him as a dutiful taskmaster, an angry traffic cop or a distant ruler. If these are your perceptions of God then your ability to enjoy the loving relationship God desires with you and between you and your spouse will never be realized. It would be as though you are trying to drive to a destination, but you couldn't read the road signs. You would get lost! As I said before, the Bible provides the road signs and markers we need to direct and fine-tune our roles and responsibilities. Praise God for the Bible and for sharing the timeless story of Abraham and Sarah!

. . . .

CHAPTER 2

God's Road Signs

G OD'S PLAN FOR marriage as outlined in Genesis was simple and specific. Man was to be responsible for the spiritual leadership of the home, and the woman was to be his helper. They were equal in ability and intelligence, but they were not equal in spiritual roles. Although "submission" has a negative tone in our feminist culture, it is a two-fold submission, and women should not feel put upon by God's directions. The husband is first responsible to God to lead his family, and then the wife is to submit to that leadership by supporting and consulting with the husband to accomplish the goal. Although the husband is in the leadership role, his accountability is directly to God.

The apostle Paul wrote in the New Testament that a husband is to "...love his wife, just as Christ loved the church and gave Himself up for her...." (Ephesians 5:22–24). Therefore, man is not to be an autocratic dictator, and a wife is not to submit to godless or sinful activity. Those instructions provide checks and balance to the marriage relationship.

In addition, God provided clarity in the form of specific roles. Husbands and wives were to have complimentary roles to one another, and together they were to have a submissive role to God. In essence, they were to operate under a divinely-fashioned organization chart. Man and woman had important roles to perform on behalf of their Creator. They were asked to follow the Creator's strategy for life by managing His creation for prosperity and nurturing a family that would continue the good things that God had put into action.

So how do we sort out all the noise, confusion, and conflict that the world is introducing into our lives and marriages?

Unfortunately, many of us manage marriage like our home-entertainment systems. We have a habit of turning on and tuning in before we read the instructions! At least, that is the way I deal with my electronic purchases! Unwrap, plug in, turn on, and then shout, "Honey, this thing doesn't seem to work!"

Have you noticed that electronic products now come with two instructions books? One is very thick and written in multiple languages. Then there is a one-page, full-color, quick-start guide with picture illustrations for those people who never will read the instructions—until they become totally discouraged and are willing to swallow their pride. Thank goodness for those quick guides, because without them, the audio/visual equipment in our home simply would be pieces of artistic technology.

So where is the marriage instruction book? Is there a quick-start guide? Fortunately, there is, and you don't have to read the whole Bible to see God's intent for marriage.

In Genesis, God stated that the married couple was to become "one flesh." Now that is not a term that we hear every day, but my friend Pastor Chip Ingram once gave an excellent metaphor of the concept of "one flesh." He described it as being two complementary pieces of Velcro that God presses together. You know Velcro very well because it has become a staple in various products, including clothing, backpacks, and automobiles. One side is soft and fuzzy, and the other has tough, plastic hooks. When you press the two sides together on something like your jacket, they form a strong bond, as though they were one piece of material or one flesh. And everyone knows the sound that Velcro makes when you try to pull it apart: *rrripppp!* It takes energy and determination to separate the "one flesh" of Velcro. It is no wonder that divorce and even break-ups of long-committed relationships are so painful and induce scars that last many years.

The interlocking concept of "one flesh" meant that the couple was to have one mindset and shared goals. And they were to depend upon God for leadership. God stated that they were to be co-rulers in the garden. I guess you could call them the first park rangers! Their complimentary gifts were to be in one accord with God's mercy and grace, which created a loving and healthy three-way relationship. It is the threefold cord that is described in Ecclesiastes 4:12: "Though one may be overpowered, two can defend themselves. A cord of three strands is not quickly broken."

The Holy Spirit in a Christian couple's life creates that third binding cord for marriage. You may be thinking that you know of happily married individuals who don't include God in their relationship. As I stated earlier, that can occur, but a marriage of two cords will end in emptiness. Humans are finite beings with an eternal soul. If you are a Christian, upon your death, your soul departs the body to reside with God. If you are not a Christian, your soul will depart and reside eternally apart from God and His love. The concept of a person remaining with us "in spirit" is a sentimental thought but one that is categorically untrue and unproven. Your loved one's spirit contacting you through a warm breeze, the flutter of butterfly wings, or the crack of thunder does not reflect what happens when a person dies. Once our spirits are freed from the earthly shackles of our bodies, we are destined to go to an eternal residence. Heaven is where Christ resides, and there the believer never again will encounter pain, discouragement, injustice, suffering, or sin. Instead, it is a place of eternal joy, contentment, glory, and fulfillment. Hell on the other hand burns with intense torment combined with the occupant's consuming regret. It is a place that you do not want to wish on your worst enemy. Hell is void of anything good or decent and is enveloped in eternal, inky darkness. Since there is no light neither God or His Son Jesus and their mercy and grace are present.

God's plan for marriage was perfect; it worked beautifully. In Scripture, He labeled it as "good." Satan's first recorded action in the Bible was his attack on marriage. In him there is nothing good. He is God's enemy. But his strategy was not to go directly after God. Instead, he started a grass-roots revolution. Satan is not the opposite of God; he is a created being who rejected God.

Satan's tactics remind me of a dolphin encounter that Terry and I shared in the Florida Keys. The instructor reminded us that we were in the dolphin's home and not to swim head to head with a dolphin. "Always swim at angles to him so that he will not consider your actions as being aggressive," stated our guide. You could die if a 300-pound dolphin swimming at eight miles per hour head-butts you!

Satan is evil, but he is not stupid. He knew that going directly at God would not work, so he attacked at an angle, with the strategy to destroy the marriage creation of God. He went after the pinnacle of God's creation: Adam and Eve. If Satan could hamper marriage, then he could interrupt and eventually destroy God's plan of reconciling Himself to people. Therefore Satan did not need to attack God directly. That is one reason the marriage covenant is under such stress and strain today and why many people without God's interaction and protection are doomed to failed marriages. Other marriages, those in which only one spouse is committed to God, face tremendous opposition when trying to retain or attain a godly focus.

Today we see the ravaging success of Satan's attacks on the family and marriage. He has developed an impressive group of accomplices in government, entertainment, the media, and even some religious organizations whose work erodes God's structure and meaning of marriage. Yet even as I key-strike these words, Satan's defeat is assured through Jesus Christ! As bad as things are in the world with Satan and his associates attacking marriage, the institution survives and thrives. Even with centuries of attacks and those who wish to redefine its meaning, God's institution continues to survive. That is not by accident, because God never breaks His promises or commitments!

Through God's Word we can be confident that the concept of the marriage covenant is a man and a woman and God. Regardless of how the government or other special interest groups spew their contempt for marriage by trying to redefine the participants, the Creator's definition of marriage has not changed just because people get comfortable with sin. God's accountability in our marriages has not changed. All men and women ultimately are accountable to the Creator, regardless of their willingness to submit to or recognize Him as such on earth. "For we will all stand before God's judgment seat. It is written: "…As surely as

I live, says the Lord every knew will bow before me; every tongue will confess to God" (Romans 14:10-11)

In Genesis 2:6–13, we read how the consequences of sin in the marriage were devastating. The sin of Adam and Eve introduced rebellion, shame, hiding, disunity, blaming, and an unhealthy fear of God into their relationship. No longer would they enjoy close, intimate walks and talks with God in the Garden. Because of sin, there was a physical and spiritual distance that began between Adam and Eve that also would carry over into their relationship with God.

Adam and Eve were naked and unashamed physically, but a relational metaphor of the word "naked" also should be considered when reading the Scripture. Without sin there were no emotional barriers in their marriage or with God. They possessed a transparency and "oneness" in their relationship with one another and with God. Sin marred those relationships, and an emotional barrier followed.

Then, because of Adam and Eve's sin, God killed animals and created the first ready-to-wear clothing. It was sin that brought about the death of sinless animals! The animals were totally blameless, but their blood was spilled. Death of an animal, death of the transparent relationship with God, and the slow and eventual death of man's body are reflections of what the Bible means when it states that "For the wages of sin is death…" (Romans 6:23). But I do not want to end with a hopeless forecast; the verse continues, "…but the gift of God is eternal life in Christ Jesus our Lord." That gift came in the form of His Son, Jesus, whose blood was spilled on the cross for our sins.

Some time after Adam and Eve first sinned, Abram and Sarai (their family names) took a journey and lived within the consequences of their actions and the constraints of an evil world. They traveled and interacted with those who had no regard for their beliefs or their God. It is a romantic-sounding adventure, but in reality, it was nomadic, lonely, dangerous, and surrounded by circumstances of uncertainty. They lived a life that was totally unlike ours, right? Wrong!

We often think our lives are boring and full of redundant actions. But consider what your life would look like if God took your story and removed the sleeping, eating, chores, and bathroom scenes and spliced it together to fit into a ninety-minute movie. Well, then viewers would have to hold onto their barrels of popcorn with both hands because of the excitement in the adventure.

When we read the Bible's limited descriptions of Abram and Sarai's lives, we often rush past the elements that make them human. That practice causes us to miss the providence of God in their lives. Maybe you think that their lives were so culturally different from yours and the era so ancient that there are no similarities and there is nothing you can learn from them. Although technology and culture changes over time, the heart remains the same. Abram and Sarai dealt with love, jealously, loneliness, hurt, disappointment, infertility, sinful decisions, and deception. There were also outsiders who wanted to rob them of precious elements in their marriage.

God asked this couple to pack up their camel and leave their network of family, friends, and conveniences and trust Him on a journey. God provided no timeframe or specified destination. It was a radical request, but God needed to make a radical change in His world. He started with the institution of marriage.

Why such a change? Maybe God needed to detoxify their marriage before He could create the nation of Israel through Him. There may have been people they relied upon who would offer the wrong kind of encouragement, and God knew they needed a clean break from that environment.

Let's discover God's plan together and find ways we can apply His timeless truth to our lives and marriages through the story of Abraham and Sarah.

CHAPTER 3

. . . .

God's Promise
(Genesis 11:27–12:3)

INITIALLY, ABRAM AND Sarai's marriage was based upon family ties and expectations. I guess you could say that they met at a family reunion! Sarai and Abram were half sister and brother. We make jokes about that today, but it was cultural and practical during that era because genetic purity provided safety in producing offspring. It wasn't until 400 years later that God commanded people not to marry their relatives.

When people think of ancient man, I am concerned that many view him through the eyes of the cultural Darwinists of our society. Talk about a bunch of people with overactive imaginations! Instead of believing that man was created carefully and with purpose, the Darwinist believes that man and woman were a cosmic accident. Thus, natural history museums want us to believe that ancient man was a lower level of human, like the caveman in the TV insurance commercials.

Just as an aside, the drawings and depictions of ancient people are totally contrived in the heads of those who want them to resemble a monkey-like species. Their goal is to support the Darwinian thinking that lower forms of creation evolved into our modern likeness. It is a false picture that has been placed in almost every museum display, but it is simply a myth like many others.

The "missing link" in Darwin's creative thinking is still missing, but your saying that comment aloud will not win you any friends or influence enemies. Godless people are fearful when their man-made science is put in jeopardy. Evolution is sitting on a rickety three-legged stool of biased assumptions, wishful thinking, and a godless worldview. When anyone ventures to challenge the theory, it is not honest science that is jostled. Instead, it is an emotional attachment to a belief system that rejects God. Weak arguments come tumbling down, and some good but godless people panic because the reality of a holy God appears in contrast to sinful and dying man.

If you lived your life believing in accidental creation and were then faced with the reality of God, you likely would understand how Dorothy must have felt when she saw behind the curtain of the mighty Oz. No longer is there the same power and intimidation that was enjoyed by the Darwinists; instead, there stands a frail, little man blowing smoke and pumping levers. It takes quite a man or woman with character to admit that he or she has spent a lifetime promoting the myth, for him or her to admit its emptiness and finally throw a carefully crafted ego of self-worth and self-made theology into the trash.

People are comfortable denying God and His theology because they mistake His love and patience when He allows them to deny His existence as an affirmation of their beliefs. As the old joke states: denial is not a river in Egypt. Nor should God's loving-kindness and mercy in your life be viewed as that of a permissive grandparent.

God created Adam and Eve genetically perfect. He gave them language, reason, and the intellectual tools needed to manage His garden. I do not know the number of generations between the creation of the first couple and the marriage of Abram and Sarai. But we read in Scripture that they were a hearty group of people living many hundreds of years. Abram's marriage to his half sister was not a genetic challenge, and it also provided the practical opportunity to maintain some cultural distinctiveness within their family.

Abram and Sarai were surrounded by pagan groups of people who practiced various abominable acts in God's eyes. We learn in Joshua 24:2 that even Terah, the father of Abram and Sarai, worshiped heathen gods. This Bible fact should be of great encouragement to us, as from it we see that God can use anyone from any family for His plans because He does not hold their past against them. God uses people "born on the wrong side of the tracks."

Additionally, we should understand and be confident in the Bible records as being the unvarnished truth of God. If the Bible were nothing more than a novel created to fool or mislead people, then the promoter of the belief system would not include shady or questionable elements of the story. Instead, the writer simply would sell the features and benefits and blame shortcomings on the victimization of people who lack adequate education and economic opportunity. But God never treats His plan or His people like victims. Rather, He reminds them that they are His creation and through Him they can accomplish great things in His name.

God had an unbelievable plan of grace to reconcile Himself to His creation through the relational vehicle of the family. He selected the brother and sister of a pagan father. And then they had severe fertility problems combined with advanced age. On paper, they were a pretty hopeless couple. Yet even though the situation was humanly impossible to fix, through God's gracious provision, Abram and Sarai would become the parents of the nation of Israel. Ultimately, through their son, Isaac, the Christ child would be born. Now that is quite a wedding gift that God sent this couple! It literally would become "the gift that keeps on giving," which indicates that Hallmark Cards may have created the marketing slogan but not the concept!

God told Abram and Sarai to do four specific things: leave their country, leave their people, leave their father's household, and go to a land He would show them. They were to leave everything they had ever known and take a tremendous leap of faith to follow God's instructions. God asked a lot from this couple and did not provide much in the way of explanation. Their response was to follow in faith one step at a time.

Maybe you can identify with their fortitude, but I am a wimp. I don't leave home without a cell phone, AAA towing card, ATM card, GPS, water bottle, and full tank of gas! My steps of faith are undergirded with personal safety nets, not to mention those that our government puts in place to protect me from myself and others. Yet the Bible records a story of Abram and Sarai's initial marriage steps—this couple's baby steps in a journey of faith that they accepted through their marriage vows and again in their willingness to respond to God's call. They held onto each other and together had little more to grasp than a bold promise from a God who said that He would "bless them." They may not have had much faith, but they were not focused on the abundance of faith; they were focused on the application of that faith.

Even with all of the noisy, pagan worship that surrounded them, God got Abram and Sarai's attention in a colorful way that made the other religious options pale in contrast. Then, in faith, and likely with a deep breath, they obeyed.

Has God gotten your attention in some way that is making you question your marriage journey, your attitude, or your approach in how you will live the remaining years you have on earth? If not, maybe you should be asking yourself this question: "Why not?" God is the same God today as He was in the Old Testament. He is actively transforming lives and marriages everyday! He wants to transform yours, but it all begins with a step of faith—and maybe a deep breath.

CHAPTER 4

Walking in Desire

I N VERSE 4 OF Genesis chapter 12, the Bible states, "So Abram went forth…" What an understatement! Their journey required a frightening "leap of faith." Contrary to the cultural norm, Abram and Sarai took the risk to leave a known and comfortable environment and to follow God. Their neighbors and family were living life and enjoying the fruits of the earth. And Abram and Sarai now would enter a pagan country and wander all their married days in a world that did not value life. It was a land where people created their own gods to meet their own selfish needs. (Hmmm, sound familiar?) When the "Welcome Wagon" came into Abram and Sarai's camp, those on the wagon encountered a couple advanced in years, unable to have children, and considered culturally cursed—a couple that was nomadic, poor, and following an unseen "god" to an unknown destination. The pitiful sight must have left onlookers shaking their heads in disbelief.

Maybe as a Christian couple you have faced similar attitudes from friends, family, and co-workers because you have chosen to live for Christ instead of mindlessly following the ways of a dying world. What then is God asking you to leave behind so that He can take you and your spouse on a marriage journey filled with grace? What is God whispering to you about today and asking you to let go of to follow Him? Can you even hear Him over all the noise and confusion of the workplace, media, traffic pattern, and the influence of your family and friends? If the answer is, "We don't know," then don't be discouraged, for you have taken the first step into seeking His will, and that step is the footfall of *desire*. When Abram and Sarai started the journey, they had a desire that they recognized only God could fulfill. In their culture, having children was a sign of success. Yet barrenness was considered a failure, bad Karma, a curse from an unknown power. They desired a baby, and they knew that God's promise of a nation being formed through them would require the birth of a child. In effect, their desire intersected with God's plan!

Their response to God's command reminds me of my favorite science fiction television show: Star Trek. Captain Picard, in the series *The Next Generation*, would select a course to an unknown world, then turn to his first officer and speak this command: "Engage." Abram and Sarai engaged God in faith and made a major change in their life. They weren't certain of the kinds of obstacles they would face, but they engaged God with their obedience and started down a path to a land that He would show them. God's command required human effort; they did not wait for God to deliver all the answers upfront. Instead, they had to pack up and begin the journey. You cannot steer a starship or a donkey cart unless it is moving, and that also goes for a marriage! Steering first requires movement. You must move forward in faith, living as God commands, because He works through His people. He works through the feet and hands of His people. God invites each of us to get involved. It is not a passive relationship; instead, it is active and dynamic.

God stated in Genesis that marriage begins with people leaving their parents, cleaving to one another, and then becoming one flesh. One flesh means more than just having sex. It also means that a couple is responding as a dance team and not stepping on one another's toes. It is about knowing how to lead, knowing how to follow, and knowing the difference!

God was a loving and graceful instructor with Abram and Sarai, and as the music played, He continued to instruct them. God did not leave them to their own interpretation. He led them and taught them through on-the-job training. It was the hard way to learn things, and we will see them succeed, fail, succeed, then fail again as we continue to review their story. But each time they created or encountered a problem, God fixed and transformed their lives because He was a major partner in their journey.

God wants to be a partner in your marriage journey, too! He wants to be the dance instructor in your marriage. It is through His Word, your prayers, and other godly people that He will teach you the dance steps and show you how to stay in rhythm.

Now, I am not much of a dancer. When I pay attention to the beat and lead properly, I do a pretty good job, and Terry has a blast. As Christian couples in this dance of life, we have to carefully listen to the rhythm and follow God; we have to listen intentionally to the beat of His song. And in my case, I have to carefully count the beat and watch my step, or I step on Terry's toes and God's metaphorical toes!

CHAPTER 5

. . . .

Healthy
Boundaries
(Scripture Focus:
Genesis 11:27–12:1–4)

IN THE SCRIPTURE passage from Genesis, we find that God instructed Abram and Sarai to leave three familiar things—their country, their people, and their father's household—and go to a land that He would show them. So what did each category require them to relinquish in order to obey God?

Leaving requires that you depart familiar terrain, hangouts, resources, and the known shortcuts. When Terry and I visit our hometown, she often will ask, "How do you know this part of town?" or "How do you know this shortcut?" Finding shortcuts became a way of life for me when we lived there because it allowed me to be in control, navigate the mundane, and hasten the trip. Departing from the well-worn ruts of your life will awaken you to every aspect of your environment and to God. You begin to see the world differently. Nothing is automatic anymore because the terrain is unfamiliar and therefore uncomfortable.

Abram and Sarai left everything and everyone they had grown to rely upon. They had to engage a new trail, and it forced them to rely on each other and turn to God for the next instruction. God did not hand them "Google Map" directions. Instead, they had to learn to walk one step at a time in faith. Uncertainty can cause anxiety, but it also can be a great blessing because it forces us to recognize that we need help. We quickly learn that we need God's provision every step of the way.

The challenge God gave them is given to every newly married couple. For God said that man is to leave his mother and father and cleave to his wife. You may never physically move very far from your hometown, but there is a physical and mental departure that a married couple must take. I will say from personal experience that leaving my hometown immediately caused me to rely more upon my wife and God rather than depending on a well-known community of friends and family. Moving away removed the temptation to rely upon old habits and resources. You may not have that opportunity because of career or other limitations, so you will have to be a bit more intentional and creative with friends and family. But don't be discouraged or think that you cannot apply these truths with your in-laws living next door. There are ways to "virtually" draw the shades on your windows so that you can have privacy with God and your spouse.

God told Abram and Sarai to leave their country. Let's recognize that the command to leave their country was in contrast with the promise, "I will make you a great nation." God was telling Abram that He would give him land in the midst of those who had an established country and way of life. That promise must have sounded impossible, but up came the tent stakes, and away they went. God told them to move into Canaan and that He would bring forth a nation of people who followed God.

Having grown up in the United States, I can visualize a little of what this situation was like. We have a country that is made up of fifty states, which are made up of counties and cities. Our home is currently in Atlanta, but I always look forward to seeing the sign along the interstate that welcomes me back to the great state of Tennessee, where we were born and raised. Next I look for the Blount Country sign and the threshold for the city of Maryville, which is our hometown. The elements that set these physical areas apart are their survey lines or "boundaries." Not only is the topography mapped by physical survey pins, but also it is controlled by differing boundary laws. For example, the state of Tennessee highway speed is 70 MPH. Blount County secondary roads are 45 MPH, and you are cautioned to reduce your speed to 35 MPH when you enter Maryville. Each area has a regulatory boundary that indicates how residents are to behave in those areas.

Abram and Sarai were nomads all of their lives, and they were told to go and make a godly nation in the midst of a pagan world. When Christians marry, we, too, are going into a pagan world in which we are to live according to the teaching of Jesus, even when the governing rules oppose Him. Therefore, our pathway to achieving a godly marriage is to live differently than the rest of the world. We must set up godly boundaries for our marriages while living inside a pagan land. Even if we do not physically leave our original zip codes, we do need to set some healthy boundaries for our marriages.

My definition of boundaries in this example is: how your marriage will operate. A state, county or city has a form of government, operating rules, and a strategy of how it will invest its resources. In our marriages, we, too, must determine our boundaries regarding how we spend our time and money and respond to the world in a godly manner.

The decision to live in this manner is an intentional decision and a departure from the way most people view marriage. "Intentional" and "departure" are the key words that tie us to the journey of Abram and Sarai. God asked them to made and act on an intentional decision by departing from their comfort zone and beginning to live according to His way.

As you step away from the influence of your family and focus on an intimate relationship with your spouse, you must create your own "family boundaries." After your pastor said, "I now pronounce you husband and wife," did you sit down and discuss your Christian marriage boundaries? If not, I encourage you to do this before you begin having children, because that event will absorb the quiet moments of sharing and discussing you enjoy when you first are married. Once you have set godly marriage boundaries, these holy boundaries will set you apart from a world of nonbelievers and you will be able to develop a foundation for marriage that you can pass onto your children.

Consider all the things God told the Israelites to do so that they would stand apart from the heathen nations. With God's direction, they set holy boundaries. For example, God said things like the following: Don't step foot on the mountain. Don't touch the ark. Don't come into the tent of the tabernacle. Don't offer sacrifices in an inappropriate method. Through these commands, God was teaching the Israelites the importance of living within healthy, holy boundaries. He gave them guardrails in their lives. But within His boundaries, they had plenty of room for movement and self-expression.

Similarly, we must set healthy, holy boundaries for our relationships, but these boundaries are not to become walls. Boundaries are healthy, like a safety railing, but I am not encouraging you to build walls between you and your family, friends, or work colleagues. I am saying that the world is not looking out for your best interests, so you had better discuss some healthy boundaries so that you and your spouse know how you will live for God. God was intentional with Abram and Sarai, so you should be specific, too.

So, what are some boundaries you need to set?

Money

One of the first discussions you should have is one about how to spend your money. All gifts come from God, and God always told His people to give back to Him. He asked for a sacrifice, and in the Old Testament, He specifically asked for 10% of the first fruits. The tithe is not a New Testament concept, so you will not find it there; instead, you will find Jesus speaking of giving sacrificially. Thus, as a couple, you should have a goal that you will give back 10% of what God gives you—not just to church, but to the missions that God places on your heart—and then give intentionally. Set aside the money, and on Sunday mornings, each of you can participate in placing the offering in the plate. (This may mean writing two checks.)

Some may say, "I pay taxes. Isn't that giving enough?" First, don't expect politicians to spend your tax dollars wisely, doing God's will, because they are not a people legislating with godly boundaries. Second, what the government takes without your permission cannot be considered a sacrificial gift to God. Jesus did not come with a political agenda. Instead, He said to "Give to Caesar what is Caesar's." And He added, "...[give] to God which is God's..." (Mark 12:17, emphasis mine). Now all things are God's, even Caesar and all past and present rulers are part of God's creation. Therefore, you are to be generous with God; He has given you all things, including your spouse! For some people, 10% isn't sacrificial, but for others, 10% is overwhelming. Yet, if

29

you give as God intends, you will set a boundary that the world cannot understand. Simply review the contribution records of public leaders in the United States. In general, you'll find many of them giving away your tax dollars, but they give nothing but lip service to any charity or to God.

Jesus said we are to, "Love the Lord your God with all your heart and with all your soul and will all your mind. This is the first and greatest commandment" (Mt. 22:37-38). One way we can show God we love Him is through the gifts that we give Him in return. Our gifts should cause us to change the way we live. If our offering has no impact on how we live our lives, then we need to increase the amount of the gift. Godly boundaries are created to change the way we live and not simply to add another rule to the playbook of life. Additionally, aside from your giving money back to God's work, I don't know of another barometer that will provide a better indicator of your spiritual journey. People's generosity with God through the use of their money provides an indicator of their relationship with Him. If it were not true, people wouldn't be so prickly about the subject of money.

Spiritual Life

The next boundary that needs to be set is related to your spiritual development. Again, it is important to focus on being intentional in your study and knowledge of God. Church should be one aspect of your journey, but you cannot expect your local church to be your spiritual Wal-Mart. That perspective is not a godly view of the body of Christ. Instead of relying solely on church, everyone should strive to find a coach or mentor. You may have heard of finding a Paul and a Timothy in your life. Those two people should be someone that you can reach down to in order to provide spiritual help (Timothy) and someone more spiritually mature, who will reach down to you (Paul). Finding the mature "Paul" is difficult and not always possible in a personal way, but there are ways to find virtual mentors. Consider finding spiritual guidance through a DVD, book, or podcast. Ask your pastor to recommend these individuals and then read their works as though they are personally mentoring you through their illustrations. It isn't as intimate as having a mentor to meet with in person, but the concept does allow you to set the time and venue for your study.

Prayer

Be intentional in your prayer life, and believe in the power of prayer. We often think that just because a prayer is not answered right away, prayer does not work. But God knows you and knows exactly what you need. Remember, His goal is not to fulfill your fleshly desires, but spiritually mold you into the likeness of His Son. Rather than making assumptions about how God is working through your prayer life, I suggest that you purchase an inexpensive notebook and record your prayers. I have found that journaling my prayers allows me to actively watch and record God's work. The activity builds my confidence and knowledge of how God works in and through my life. It also allows me to reflect upon my requests and, in turn, strive to follow God's will instead of my selfish agenda. The practice also encourages me to move away from petition into gratefulness. "Be joyful always; pray continually; give thanks in all circumstances, for this is God's will for you in Christ Jesus." (1 Thes. 5:16-18)

Pray as a couple at least once a week. Set a date and time, and stick to your prayer commitment time to God and your spouse. Prayer works, but it is not to be rote begging.

Prayer is your time with God simply to speak to Him in your language. You do not need to talk to God like you are reading a legal document or the King's English; instead, make it a time of recognizing God's greatness.

You should begin by letting God know that you appreciate His role in creation, your life, and the sustaining power of all things that exist. Christians often pray as though what we have been given is the threshold of expected provision and it is God's responsibility to layer on more stuff. For example, Jesus stated in the Lord's Prayer that we are to ask for "daily bread." When you ask God for daily nourishment, you recognize that what you received yesterday isn't automatically what you will have today or tomorrow. Each thing we receive is a gift from God.

After you have given thanks to God, then you naturally will speak to those needy issues that are on your heart. If you worship God first and thank Him for His gifts, then your requests for help will take on a different tone. You'll slowly begin learning to pray in God's will, and those are the kinds of prayers that get answered!

Service

Where will you spend your time in service to God? I don't believe in developing guilt trips or arm-twisting tactics to gain volunteers for projects. How people spend their money and time speaks to the kind of relationship they have with God. Let's admit it, unbelievers are good social volunteers too, and many are better at it than Christians! So let's make certain that we allow God to use us for *His* ministry rather than creating service ministries ourselves and using His name as an endorsement.

I have seen firsthand that through the power of Christ, God raises up volunteers for His service. In the Bible study class I teach, I have witnessed God-driven people asking me to serve in various roles and create service ministries. God did the prompting in their lives because they were putting themselves in the path of God through Bible study, prayer, and small group accountability. You'll find the same thing will happen for you. If you as a couple don't have a ministry, then ask yourself, "Why?" God wants you to be involved in His mission work. He works through His creation and those who love and follow Him. He wants to work in you individually and through your marriage.

Intentional Living

Planning your life around intentionally pursuing God's purpose for your marriage will set you apart in a godless world. Let me encourage you to consider doing an annual planning meeting with your spouse. Terry and I have done this for twenty-five years. Granted, some years have been more effectively evaluated and planned than others, but the time invested has resulted in blessings in our marriage because God was included in the planning process.

I have placed a planning sheet in the appendix of this book for your consideration. It provides the topics and categories of your life that you should discuss and dream about annually! One indirect blessing you will receive from the process is the activity of communicating as a couple and with God. It should take you a number of weeks to complete the process individually, and then you can come together to discuss the final document. You will be blessed not only because you planned and accomplished the task, but also because God will surprise and bless you beyond your plans and tasks!

CHAPTER 6

A Home of
Their Own

T HE NEXT STEP of Abram and Sarai's departure required that they leave their father's household. OK, this one won't be especially easy because the departure is as equally emotional as it is physical. Many of you already have left your hometowns, just like Terry and I did. We grew up in a small town, where many of the people never move more than a few miles away from their parents. Yet even in transient Atlanta, there are couples living far from home who remain closer to their parents in relationship than they do to their spouse, and certainly closer than they are to God. Sometimes physical distance is bridged with emotional fixes, and that is a prescription for a weak marriage; it thwarts the kind of relationship God intends for you.

Terry and I recently hosted a marriage panel for our class. We used three couples: married fifty years, married twenty-five years, and married fifteen years. The subject the eldest married couple on the panel first introduced to the class was the need to control visits and avoid drop-ins.

This couple, who had been married fifty years and had grandchildren, came at the subject from the in-laws' viewpoint instead of from the eyes of the newlyweds. They told us that they treated their children's family the way they would have wanted their in-laws to treat them when they first got married. They believed that there must be a respect for the new family. They believed that in-laws should, "out of courtesy and respect," telephone ahead to make an appointment for a visit. Sitting in the driveway and using the cell phone doesn't count!

It may be that your in-laws are not as generous and proactive in creating this respectful boundary. Your job may be more difficult because of the potential for hurting someone's feelings. Physically leaving town automatically provides a solution to this situation and avoids the potential for emotional misunderstandings.

Consequently, this boundary also should extend to "night-night" phone calls. I have a friend whose mother called every night to say "good night" to her baby boy— that is, every night throughout his *first* marriage that unfortunately ended in divorce. His wife never felt "clung to" because her husband was still clinging to momma. In a sense, he never had left his father's household.

We recently spent the weekend with my college mentor and his wife. Jim was the commander of the Air Force ROTC detachment at the University of Tennessee, and I was once one of his cadets. During our visit, they presented us with a sign stating, "Always Kiss Me Goodnight." They said that it was one of the reasons they have enjoyed a long and loving relationship. We have the sign in our bedroom, and it reminds me that if you can kiss your spouse goodnight, then you are not going to bed angry. Does that mean everything is always sunshine and roses and that you never have arguments? Goodness, no! Maybe this happens in the movies but not in real life. The sign reminds me that Terry is the most important girl in my life and that our relationship defines our lives and our relationship with God. Since God ordained our marriage and gave me a wonderful partner, it is important that at the close of each day I honor both God and Terry through a loving relationship.

Responsibilities

Life is full of responsibilities and challenges. Each day we are not only met with the mundane activities, but also we are surprised with stuff that breaks, leaks, needs medical attention, or requires a payment. Those events give you opportunities to rely upon your spouse, your first mate!

I will never forget the time we decided to lay a new kitchen floor. We went to the tile store and bought all the needed supplies. "It will be easy," the salesman told us. So first thing Saturday morning, we got to work on the project. When we moved the refrigerator, we encountered a rotting hole in the floor. Many years of a leaky icemaker had ruined the subfloor. I called the tile store, and the associate replied, "Just lay a new subfloor over the top and you'll be fine." Lay a new floor over the top? Now that advice was "over the top," as we had no clue how to attempt that project. I remember we sat down on the floor and looked at each other, wishing we had gone to the lake instead of starting this project. Now it was too late to push the refrigerator back into place because I had torn up the linoleum. Our parents lived four hours away, and even if they lived in the same town, they wouldn't know how to lay a subfloor.

Terry said, "Let's go to Home Depot and get the supplies." We did, and by the end of the weekend, we had a beautiful new kitchen floor. Not only did we accomplish the task of building a floor, but also we built on our relationship of trust and teamwork. The blessing of fixing stuff together gives you practice for dealing with important decisions that intersect with your life. The communication you invest in during those times will provide you with positive roadmaps for communicating when making future decisions and working through issues.

Terry and I also have encountered times when our communication was poor and our solution became an expensive mistake. One such story involves our purchase of deck furniture. Each of us was convinced that the other person wanted a certain group of furniture. I negotiated the price, and Terry determined the delivery. Upon its arrival, I stated, "I'm glad we were able to get something that you really wanted."

Terry replied, "I never wanted this; I thought you did."

We discovered that neither one of us wanted the product for ourselves but we mistakenly had wanted it for the other person! It was clear we loved one another, but we were not communicating effectively. So through that experience, we have coined a phrase that we still use at decision times: "Is this another deck furniture purchase?" We always take those decisions before God, but He is very generous and allows us a lot of freedom to make some good and bad decisions.

I recommend that you find a special phrase you can say to your spouse that only you two and God will know the meaning of. The phrase's purpose is to remind each person to evaluate his or her agenda and motivation for a decision. King David spoke a prayer that reflects that thought in Psalm 139:23–24: "Search me, O God, and know my heart; test me and know my anxious thoughts. See if there is any offensive way in me, and lead me in the way everlasting."

Finances

I recently was listening to Clark Howard's radio show, and he was advising a young married couple to seek funding from the "Bank of Mom and Dad." He stated that the parents likely would not require collateral and the interest rate would be low. There may be emergency times in your life, such as a health issue, that will require you to approach your parents for money, but if at all possible, avoid making that decision. Clark's advice was sincere but sincerely wrong. The Bank of Mom and Dad requires collateral and interest. When parents start writing checks on your behalf, then they have an interest in how the money is spent and when it will be repaid. They may be generously saying "not to worry," but they are human, especially when it comes to money. Over time, your relationship with the Bank of Mom and Dad can become strained.

I have worked for and with banks for twenty-five years, as has Terry. We have witnessed that customers initially are excited to borrow money for a product they cannot afford, but over time, the monthly payments to the bank become a burden. Borrowers know the money is theirs to repay, but as the asset ages and the value declines, the same loan payment continues to be due on the 15th or 30th of the month. The beloved banker becomes another dreaded "bill in the mailbox" that limits the borrower's lifestyle and living expenses.

You do not want to get into that kind of "banking" relationship with your parents. Their gifts are a different story, but remember, there are no free lunches. We live in a society where unethical politicians constantly promise "free lunches," but nothing in life is free—nothing. Your parents likely funded your education and wedding and have made a huge investment and sacrifice in raising you. Now, be a good steward of their investment and get off the payroll! Love them and allow them to love you without continuing to write checks. If they fund your debt, then they are owed their expectations, and that is fair. "No strings attached" is seldom a realistic offer because people are human (even well-meaning parents). The "string" that led you to the front door of the Bank of Mom and Dad also stretches back from their checkbook to your front door. If you must have a banking transaction with them, then have a written agreement with terms and conditions, or better yet, hire a company to send you a monthly bill. If for some reason you have no other option than to borrow from your mom and dad, then pay them back sacrificially, and never put them into a position of being your debt collectors. You'll have many debt collectors in this world, but only one set of parents. Honor them and honor God.

One good friend of ours told his children, "I cannot borrow for my retirement, but you can borrow for your education." Sacrifice before you borrow from parents, and parents, allow your children the lesson and gift of sacrificial living. Invest in your family by sacrificing, even if that means the luxury vacation you desire ends up being a camping trip. One of the first vacations Terry and I took was a camping trip along the coast of California. It was a last-minute fly/drive deal filled with great times and Pop-Tarts for breakfast! That sacrifice built memories and strengthened our bond. We learned how to accomplish things with less money, and we also learned how to save. Later on, when we wanted a new car, we drove only one car until we could afford to buy the new one with cash. I still remember our carpooling to and from work in the mornings and afternoons. We built great memories of sacrifice.

Arguments

Never introduce parents into an argument or ask them to referee. You should ask your parents to hang up the phone or close the front door, unless the argument could result in a dangerous situation of physical harm. Couples should cry to each other and God first, not to Momma and Daddy. The Bible states, "Blessed are the peacemakers." One of my seminary professors reminded me that the Bible never stated, blessed are the peace*keepers*. Making peace requires dealing with difficult situations and working out those differences in "truth and love." If you invest in working out differences with your spouse, without parental referees and with a godly attitude, your marriage will grow strong and prosper.

Traditions

Create your own traditions for holidays and special celebrations or vacations. Make yourselves a family by merging your separate traditions into a blending or by taking turns doing what your family "used to do." Then find a way to make the tradition yours. Invite your extended family to your house for celebrations rather than trying to determine whose mother's house you'll visit during those emotional times of Christmas and Thanksgiving. Just because you've done it that way for twenty years as a single person in your father's household, doesn't mean it needs to continue once you are married. Your children will want the comfort of family traditions. Having them gives you the opportunity to model how God is consistent and can be relied upon in their lives. Also, finding the proper boundaries will make your visits back home even more meaningful. Your parents will begin to respond to you as a family unit instead of as "her husband" or "his wife." Your modeling this kind of Christian leadership will be difficult, lonely, and initially stressful, but the long-term blessings and boundaries will produce fruit in your marriage.

Safety

There is one family situation, regardless of traditions and expectations, that must be addressed carefully, and that is one of safety. The role of the husband is the protector of the wife, as God designed. The wife is to be the helper to the husband as they work together to follow God's plan. If there is an unhealthy and unsafe extended family relationship, then that situation must be avoided. Do not put your spouse in a vulnerable circumstance simply for the sake of family expectations. You must control the access or schedule meetings in safe, public venue. We can love and respect our extended families, but God calls us to cling to each other as one flesh, and that also means protecting and supporting our spouse.

Family Chaplain

It is too easy to slip into the role of family chaplain or missionary, especially if you are a Christian and the members of your extended family are not. But I suggest that you pray and discuss this challenging "opportunity" with your spouse. One difficult group of people Jesus had to deal with was His own family. They just couldn't accept that He was the Messiah, and yet they had known Him all His life. Don't try to change your family, unless God calls you into that position. Pray for them, love and support them, but recognize that your marriage has only three strands that make up the rope of a godly marital relationship. You can set an example for them, but preaching to them seldom wins any converts.

There is an old business joke that asks, "What is the difference between an employee and consultant?" Answer: About 100 miles. Managers seldom listen to employees, but they will pay a consultant big money to come into town to tell them the same story. That scenario plays out in family dynamics too. I think Dave Ramsey, the Christian financial counselor, calls it "the powdered butt syndrome." He wisely states, "Your parents don't want to take advice from people whose butt they used to powder" (*Financial Peace Revisited*, pg. 233). Fortunately, you still can love them all the way to the cross!

Friends

God told Abram and Sarai to "leave your people"; in other words, leave your old friends. The friends you had when you were single may or may not continue to be your "marriage friends." It takes work to find couple friends— hard work and patience. Terry and I have experienced that the dynamic of getting together with spouses can be challenging sometimes. For example, we have had dinner dates with couples where Terry connects with the wife and I have zero in common with the husband, apart from our shoes resting under the same table. Be patient, persistent, and prayerful, and you will find new friends as a couple.

Consequently, this pursuit also requires that the guy's night and girl's night out routines cease. You can maintain friendships, but don't hang with the singles crowd like you did in the past. Make an intentional break, and focus your interests on your spouse and building a godly relationship.

In addition, don't allow friends too much "Dear Abby" access into your life. Some friends have unhealthy agendas and hurts that they want you to embrace or affirm. They may bring their relationship problems into your life and begin to look for commonality with you. I know of a woman who was divorced, and within five years, her two closest friends were divorced, too. They informally formed a "My Man Done Me Wrong Club." Just remember that sincere old friends can be sincerely wrong. You must seek out godly wisdom. If your friends are not Christians who submit their lives unto Christ, then their advice, as sound as it may seem, will not have the wisdom that God offers believers. There are some toxic people in this world who just want to bring you into their problematic domain so that you can share in their misery.

Setting boundaries with friends will create some tension, especially if you also are breaking ungodly habits that they are retaining. Hurt feelings can ensue and so will misunderstandings. They might feel left out, and you might feel left out! But I encourage you to maintain integrity in all aspects of your life. Being honest in your relationships with friends means not saying one thing and then doing another. Remind your friends that your goal is having a godly marriage that lasts. Maintaining a godly marriage in the midst of your friends may be your only witnessing opportunity to lead them to Christ.

. . . .

CHAPTER 7

Just Do...
God's Will

A FTER THE LORD explained what Abram and Sarai were to leave behind, He then said, "...go to a land I will show you." His message was in the future tense, meaning that they were to leave without being certain of their destination. They therefore would lead a nomadic life and remain on the move in order to be obedient to those words God spoke to them. Although much of God's message was specific, the directions required that they take a step of faith. There is an old saying, "You cannot steer a bike until the wheels are rolling." Abram and Sarai were submitting themselves to God's direction, and they began by moving forward with certainty and their trust of God, but they were uncertain as to where He would take them.

Most of us make elaborate plans as to how and where we will live. In fact, we agonize over our career decisions and often ponder if we are fulfilling what God has called us to accomplish during our lifetime. We would be considered by the world to be foolish to head out without a destination in mind, but God calls us to live and walk in faith. God isn't asking us to make the same physical journey as Abram and Sarai, but He asks that we obey His commands and trust Him. When we do so, He will guide us to the destination that will be good for us and glorify Him.

Your immediate response may be, "But God isn't telling me do anything specific," or "I haven't heard His voice." Have you ever imagined what it would be like actually to hear God's voice from heaven? Would it thunder like a stadium announcer or speak mildly as a counselor? Would God's voice scare you so that you could not move, or would you be willing to drop everything for Him and respond? God speaks to us through the Bible, His Son Jesus, and affirming communication from the Holy Spirit. You may never hear God "call an audible," but His hand in your life can be recognized and be a catalyst for your faithful response. The journey of Abram and Sarai illustrates that God focused on the development of their character. He used their life experiences as the delivery vehicle for testing them, educating them, and helping them to build a lasting relationship with Him

When I was in fifth grade, I visited the Huntsville Space and Rocket Center. The building was full of gleaming aircraft displays. Even sitting still, they looked fast. Later that night after I returned home and crawled into bed I dreamed of climbing into cockpits and soaring into outer space. How I wish I could have had the hands-on exploration that kids today enjoy through space camp!

In essence, God provided Abram and Sarai a hands-on, interactive relationship through their marriage journey. The fact that they were nomadic illustrates that the location of their tent pegs was not as important to God as where their hearts were planted. Regardless of your current occupation or location, God can use you and your spouse if you make yourselves available to Him. God has a plan for your marriage. His Word tells us to walk before Him in faith, not knowing what we will encounter but knowing our ultimate destination is to be with Him forever.

If you are a young married couple, you still may be enjoying the "honeymoon glow," or you may be a few years past that point now. Regardless of the amount of time you have been together, you share many of the same circumstances and uncertainties that faced Abram and Sarai. They were not certain what God had in mind for their finances, health, career, investments, home, or the big uncertainty, children! They had fertility problems, but God promised to make a nation of people from them. Their fertility issue would have to be addressed. Married couples today are facing many uncertain economic, health, and relationship issues. To successfully tackle this journey with a sense of joy, you are going to need a great relationship with God and your spouse. You will need healthy communication and a religious foundation that will prepare you for the emotional roller coasters of your journey together.

So where do you begin? With faith in Jesus Christ, you take the first step! In verse 4 of Genesis Chapter 12, the Bible records, "So Abram left…" This couple was uncertain as to what God had in store for them, but they used the faith they possessed and loaded up their belongings and faced a world that did not value life or respect their obedience to God. They clung to an unbelievable promise from God—a promise as unbelievable as the promise God makes to us for having faith in Jesus Christ! In essence, God invited them to become a partner in the gospel message that would bring forth the Savior of the world. The Lord said, "I will bless you. I will make your name great, and you will be a blessing. I will bless those who bless you and whoever curses you I will curse; and all peoples on earth will be blessed through you." God's promise required mental and emotional perseverance and that they think bigger than they ever had before. They did not have a complete grasp of God's promise; that is illustrated by some of the mistakes they made along the way. God promised to bless them and those who treated them well. Great faith would be followed by great rewards.

God rewards those who believe and act upon His Word by faith and apply that faith every day. For us, it means taking the Sunday school lessons beyond the church front door and living them out so that the world will see a difference our in marital journey. That lesson is easier said than done! It was for Abram and Sarai. They were advanced in age, a little discouraged, and likely concerned about the future. Sarai was beyond childbearing years, but a child remained at the center of their marriage plans. A baby was the desire of their hearts, but their agenda would be tested before their dream would be realized.

Since they had no children to help with work, Abram took his nephew Lot with him. Lot would be a trusted helper in the family business as well as a practical solution for Abram's need for an heir. Lot was the fallback plan if God did not provide a child. Although Abram and Sarai believed God, they had not experienced His unlimited ability to provide for their lives and specifically to heal a barren woman. So they played it safe, just in case God did not meet their expectations. They exercised the faith they had, and that is all God asks of us.

Christ once told a parable about three workers who were given five, two, and one talent to invest in the landowner's kingdom. Each man who invested what he had was praised, but the one who fearfully did not invest the gift was disciplined. God shows that He rewards our faithful journey, regardless of its initial distance.

Genesis 12:8 states that Abram built an altar in the midst of a pagan people, in a foreign land, to honor God. Then he "...called on the name of the Lord." Luther translated the word "called" as preached. But would Abram practice what he preached? Many times after a person's bold proclamations in support of God, the individual is tested. For example, Jesus told Peter after one of his bold proclamations, "Satan wants to sift you but I have prayed for you." Abram and Sarai moved forward in their walk with God, but their faith would be tested. The testing began during a circumstance that impacted them and their idol worshiping neighbors.

According to Genesis 12:10, a famine swept the land. Crops would be destroyed and grazing land would be limited. This famine was the first recorded in the Bible, but many others would follow. In fact, one would touch a great grandchild of Abram, a man named Joseph. (You can read more about Joseph beginning in Genesis 37.) It was the duty of an Egyptian ruler to plan ahead for these occurrences and to protect people from starvation, so Abram and Sarai responded to the situation by entering the territory of Egypt to obtain the needed supplies. As indicated in Chapter 12, verses 4–8, Abram and Sarai were God's first missionaries in the foreign, pagan land.

At this time, Sarai was about age sixty-five. The Bible states that she was still young-looking and beautiful. Beauty in that time often was an observation of the qualities of the skin, eyes, and hair. The name Sarai means "princess," which may be a description of her physical attractiveness or the nature of her personality. Typically, the mother named the baby, and the ancient world believed that a name expressed the essence of an individual. Babies often were named with hope that the verbal descriptor would become a prophetic expression of the character and destiny of the child. Later in Abram and Sarai's story, God changed their names, which revealed that they'd had a transformation of character.

At age sixty-five, Sarai was in her prime, but her beauty was a challenge for Abram. He knew that the Egyptians respected marriage. Therefore he believed the Egyptians would kill him so that they might deliver her to the Pharaoh as a gift. Abram was the spiritual leader of the family, and His role was to trust God and walk righteously before Him. Unfortunately, Abram decided to lie about Sarai and say she was his sister instead of admitting that she was his wife. In doing this, he demonstrated that he did not recognize her as a gift, but in this circumstance, he saw her as a liability. He was selfish, and his actions indicated that he cared more for his life than his wife. She was treated as a possession instead of the soul mate God had intended when He created man and woman for marriage.

Now Sarai truly was his half-sister. But first and foremost and in the eyes of God, she was fully his wife. Half-truths indicate the presence of half-lies, and somehow Abram was able to rationalize lying to men and asking his wife to affirm the lie. Maybe he figured that Sarai would be well taken care of in the harem. Life in a harem was not like a Hollywood movie plot. The women were well cared for and would remain in household protection until their death. Maybe Abram reasoned that God would rescue Sarai from this situation, but lying and scheming do not reflect godly leadership in a husband.

It is understandable that they were facing an intimidating and dangerous circumstance and felt vulnerable before a powerful and pagan nation. Fear clouded Abram's judgment, but his fear indicated a lack of faith in God. When man's fear encounters a difficult or uncertain circumstance, then the combination will lead to poor decisions. Abram's scheme actually jeopardized God's promise and risked Sarai's life and character in the process. If the Pharaoh had had sex with Sarai, even if she later became pregnant by Abram, there would always be a question as to who the child's father was. Remember the earlier reference to Satan's indirect threat to God's plan of redemption through marriage and family? 1 Peter 5:8 states, "Your enemy the devil prowls around like a roaring lion looking for someone to devour." Satan will use the world and its resources to create fear in your life and lead you into making decisions that illustrate your lack of faith and plunge you deep into despair. That kind of despair is rooted in a distrust of God, leads to distrust of your spouse, and often is followed by strained relationships and even divorce.

Sitting in our comfortable chairs, it is easy to second-guess Abram and Sarai's situation and imagine how we would have made a better decision. Yet we will only make wise and discerning decisions when faith in God looms larger than life's circumstances. The journey to wealthy Egypt was attainable for Abram and Sarai, but God's promise seemed out of reach for them. The couple never imagined that God would gift them with their own child at their advanced ages. What a mess they made while trying to fix their problems apart from God's direction! Now they needed God's assistance in an even greater way.

Even though your marriage will not be confronted by the same circumstances as Abram and Sarai's, there may be times that the pressures of a sinful world will cause you to make poor marital decisions. Decisions that do not reflect a trust in God lead to sin, guilt, and regret. You must be prayerful about your decisions and recognize that your decisions can negatively impact your marriage and the good gifts that God wants to provide.

In the past, I have allowed fear to lead my decision-making process. Fear has caused me to make poor career decisions and jeopardize my family. I have allowed fear to drive financial decisions that I regretted for years, and it caused my family and me great stress. I did not suffer in solitude, because families suffer together. Again, we must remember that sin is not really secret, and it is not simply a personal thing that does not impact others. Thankfully, God was merciful and rescued me from myself!

God will rescue you too! And God rescued Sarai. Ultimately, Abram was handed wealth from the Pharaoh, Abram's life was preserved, and he received his wife back without a fight. God was merciful and a loving provider, even to sinful people who did not deserve His loving-kindness. He loves all unconditionally, and that kind of love is not something you can experience without the presence of God. Through having Christ in your life, you, too, can love your spouse and others unconditionally. Apart from God you can experience many kinds of love that often borders on sentimentality, but unconditional love is available only for those who have a personal relationship with Jesus Christ.

It is easy to classify yourself as a faithful person when you obey God knowing there is something to gain. But it is difficult when you are afraid and uncertain of the outcome. In God's eyes, faithfulness means that you obey Him regardless of the circumstances and without calculating the outcome. Abram's strategy was to save his own skin and profit from the world's sinful ways. In essence, Abram told Sarai, "Lie so I will be treated well." Through God's merciful interaction, Pharaoh ultimately did treat him well. Sarai the sister was a way for Abram to gain his short-term salvation and financial gain in the world (Egypt). But in God's eye's, Sarai the wife was the means to eternal salvation for the world and a treasure in heaven!

Sarai was willing to go along with her husband's lie to protect his life. Maybe she felt a sense of duty as a wife and trusted Abram over God. We also could think that she didn't object because of their culture, but that concept gets nullified later in their story. Subsequent verses illustrate that Sarai had a mind of her own in relation to her handmaiden Hagar. Maybe she bought into the idea that Lot would be their heir. Then again, maybe she had started believing the wagging tongues of the world that spoke of her barren condition. Enduring the demeaning situation over the years may have worn her down. It seems that being barren, having a lack of self-esteem, and living in a new land with no family, a famine, and the intimidation of evil authority figures was too much to overcome for a person who was just getting to know God.

During this era, barren women were thought to be cursed or out of favor with God or the pagan gods. Infertility is a condition that connects your generation to that of Abram and Sarai. But barren does not mean worthless; it means not ready. For example, a desert is barren until the right conditions occur. Then desert flowers will bloom, and grass will grow. Simply visit Palm Desert, California, and see for yourself. If you give living water to a desert, it will flourish. Palm Desert is filled with green golf courses and manicured yards.

Today's healthcare advances have provided many medical options for women that never were imagined only a few years ago. But with these great advances also come ethical questions and challenges that are difficult to address. It seems that discoveries come faster than we can evaluate the long-term consequences. Simply having the ability to perform a procedure does not make it an action that is acceptable to God. If you are dealing with infertility or any health issue, I encourage you to be prayerful, carefully research the options, and have godly mentors you can rely upon for feedback. Many medical solutions are easily acceptable, while others should pose an ethical challenge for God's people. Be skeptical of physicians' advice because they have a vested interest in how you spend your time and money. Their job is to push the world's medical envelope, but our role is to stay within God's holy boundaries. Therein lay the conflict that Abram and Sarai faced when they crossed over the boundary of Egypt. Although they worshiped the King of Creation, the king of Egypt was a pagan and in possession of needed food. Yet God is in control of all things—even a Pharaoh!

After Abram and Sarai lied, Sarai was taken into Pharaoh's palace. Then God caused Pharaoh's house to experience problems, or plagues, as described in the Bible. Therefore Abram and Sarai's sin to deceive the Pharaoh's men impacted Abram and Sarai's marriage, their relationship with God, and non-believers. We live in a world where non-believers say that sin is OK if no one gets hurt. The truth is that anytime there is dishonesty, someone always gets hurt. In fact, God's Word says, "Against you [God], you only, have I sinned; I have done what is evil in your sight...." (Psalm 51:4).

Pharaoh was a superstitious man and noticed that the problems his house encountered coincided with Sarai's joining the harem. The Pharaoh was no nice guy, but even he asked Abram, "Why didn't you tell me she was your wife?" Although Sarai and Abram were the godly ones, it was the pagan Pharaoh who challenged their deceptive strategy. Then the Pharaoh confronted their dishonesty by commanding them to get out of his country. God's missionaries had not proven themselves faithful. Ironically, they had plotted and schemed just like any pagan living in Egypt. The decisions they made destroyed their ability to witness for God, and they were shown a one-way road out of town.

Just like Abram and Sarai, our ability to witness for
God can be hampered by our decisions and lifestyles.
Living a life of integrity means that our response to life's
circumstances is applied both in church and in the world.
The perception of the world is that Christians are hypocrites,
so let's not contribute to that belief through our poor or
sinful decisions.

Abram and Sarai did not see or believe that God had a
specific plan for their marriage. They became impatient and
allowed circumstances to lead their decisions. Uncertainty
clouded their judgment and their lack of faith caused them
to sin, negatively impacting their marriage. As a husband,
Abram was not being a good steward of the helper that God
had provided him, and Sarai willingly went along with the
lie. Submissiveness to her husband was God's plan, but
she was not submissive in a way that would glorify God.
Instead, she participated in deception. A lie is a lie—you
cannot do the wrong thing for the right reason, so count
the cost of your decisions.

God had made Abram and Sarai a promise, and God
keeps His promises. God has not spoken to any of us in
the context or with the intent that He spoke to Abram and
Sarai. Clearly His mission for them was unique. But we
know that God, through Jesus Christ, wants to bless us as
spiritual offspring of Abraham and Sarah. It was through the
seed of Abraham that the sins of the world were forgiven.
We are the benefactors of God's grace, just as Sarai and
Abram were benefactors of His grace. They did not deserve
anything they received. God plucked them out of obscurity
and used them to bless the world for an eternity.

In your marriage, God will give you the opportunity
to learn the meaning of faithfulness. He will allow you to
scheme and make mistakes and will then be faithful to lead
you out of the bondage of the sin to which you essentially

sold yourself. You will not avoid the consequences of your actions, but God forgives and wants a close relationship with you.

As a married couple, you are going into, in the midst of, or coming out of a difficult circumstance. You will discover that you have options and decisions to make. The world will seem confusing and always willing to lead you into a godless solution. You may be fearful and uncertain of what you should do next. How then do you make godly decisions while living through a financial, relational, or even health famine?

Your first step is to know God's Word and apply it to your marriage. You and your spouse are now one flesh and members of God's marriage covenant and His eternal family in Christ. You are Christian sojourners in a pagan land that is ruled by the prince of darkness, Satan. The world is evil, and you are God's missionaries. You are not missionaries by occupation, but as Christians, you are God's hands and voice in a world that does not know Him. Therefore you are on-mission for God. God calls you to live your life as Christ taught, and having a godly marriage may be your greatest and most vocal testimony. Let me assure you that if you remain married for the long haul, you will be noticed! Just as others noticed that Abraham stacked up the stones and made a physical altar, your community will notice that you are Christians living as God intended. You don't stack stones and build altars to God. Instead, your commitment to God through loving Him is the "altar" you and your spouse build in a pagan land.

God intended that a man and a woman would live together as married people, not like the Pharaoh, who lived with women. Pharaoh's way of "living together" now has become acceptable even to Christians. Living together outside of marriage amounts to little more than a convenient roommate arrangement. But God's covenant is not simply a circumstantial promise. He is not bound by time and space like mortal man. He views a covenant as both promise and accomplishment at its implementation.

The catalyst for most people living together is either financial or sexual. That arrangement does not reflect a commitment nor is it what God desires for man and woman. It is a sin. There isn't a literal Pharaoh who wants to steal your spouse, but there is Satan, who wants to destroy what God has joined together: your marriage! He often will disguise distractions as blessings. To accomplish this task, there will be temptations for job offers, financial opportunities, time-absorbing hobbies, and avocations that can rob your relationship of joy. Not to mention that you may be tempted to have a relationship with someone outside of your marriage. If you are not careful then, like Abram, you will justify your decisions and actions. Maybe not at first, but the more you entertain actions that God would not condone, the more comfortable you will become in selecting solutions where the ends justify the means.

Ironically, you may even make some poor decisions because you love your family. The desire to provide for one's family can result in turning one's focus away from God and toward more money, a new job, and a new life. Abram's desire to provide for his family during a famine was not a mistake. God calls us to care for and provide for our families, and both Christians and non-Christians often share the same needs and desires. Just as the famine impacted all people in the region in Abram's era, financial, political, and cultural famines impact Christians and non-Christians alike. Yet the Christian must not do the wrong thing for the right reason. The Bible tells us that a man is to love his wife as Christ loves the church (Ephesians 5:25). Christ died to create the church, so man is left with a great lifestyle example and the God-given responsibility of being the head of the household.

Men have to realize in a respectful way that women are the weaker sex. In this feminist-influenced world, that statement is counter to some people's belief system and viewed as offensive. Yet men and women are different because they were created to complement one another. For example, a man doesn't enter dimly-lit parking garages fearing for his sexual purity. Women are targets for predators and are vulnerable in a way that men respectfully need to keep in the forefront of their minds.

Women are to be submissive to their husbands. In this chapter's example, I do not think that Sarai showed a godly submission; instead, she was convinced to lie. If a woman is presented with an immoral, illegal, or sinful decision, then she should not comply with her husband's wishes. The Bible records that Abram talked to Sarai about the situation in Egypt. After a discussion, she agreed. But we also know from Scripture that Sarai had a mind of her own, as illustrated in her interactions with God and Abram. She laughed when God stated that she would have a child and then lied, saying that she did not laugh. She was pushy with Abram and insisted he impregnate her maidservant. My point is that Sarai always had the ability to be honest because she illustrated that she was not intimidated to speak her mind on issues that she found important. Her role as a submissive wife was to help Abram see that sin in any form was not God's plan for their marriage.

In a sinful world, even the best decisions that are based on prayer and godly advice may not work out as you expect. The reason that happens is something that I label "evil constraint." Evil sometimes constrains our ability to do exactly as we desire, but we must be committed to following God's direction regardless. Walking faithfully with God will be rewarded. God will provide for and take care of those who love Him. Sarai and Abram were thrown out of the country, but God kept their marriage intact, protected Sarai, and blessed them. Blessings are not always financial. In fact, eternal blessings have little to do with money, but that doesn't exclude God's willingness to bless you financially also. Pharaoh gave Abram wealth as a way of trying to rectify his mistake. God controlled even the superstitious and pagan Pharaoh! The experience with God coming to their rescue should have bolstered Sarai and Abram's faith and trust in God's Word. The journey continued and so did their on-the-job training. So will yours!

. . . .

CHAPTER 8

Speed Bumps
(Genesis 16:1–16)

A FTER THE FAMINE-DRIVEN visit into Egypt, ten years elapse in the Bible narrative of Sarai and Abram's marriage journey. Although the Pharaoh forced them out of his country, they left with the wealth of livestock, Egyptian slaves, field hands, silver, and gold. Their nephew Lot was doing pretty well, too. So well that he decided to leave the family business and begin his own venture. Up to this point, Abram had been his mentor and senior business partner. Lot had watched how Abram built his livestock business and was now ready to branch out on his own instead of working in the shadow of his aunt and uncle.

When Lot suggested they divide the herds, Abram was gracious and gave him the choice of any parcel of grazing land he desired. Lot saw the rich fields of the Jordanian plain and the wealth and commercial growth in the towns of Sodom and Gomorrah. The towns embraced the cultural attitude of diversity and progressive thinking, and they were popular places to live. The Bible records that the citizens followed their own sense of moral and ethical standards. Abram continued to worship God and grow in knowledge and faith, and God recognized him as righteous. Unlike Abram, who had been called by God to leave his country, family, and people, Lot had no such call on his life. Instead, Lot surveyed the options and departed to live among those who purposefully engaged in sin, which made them enemies of God.

Choice grazing land was the lifeblood of Abram's business, and the Bible records that every well Abram dug provided water. God rewards righteous living, but that doesn't mean that you will avoid work, calloused hands, and sweating behind a shovel. You may think you are in a barren, waterless land, but just under the crusty surface, God has provision for you. At a time when most men might be second guessing their decision to give the choice grazing land away, God spoke to Abram. He reminded Him of the promise and said to stop standing around second-guessing himself, "Go, walk through the length and breadth of the land, for I am giving it to you" (Gen. 13:17).

When we do the right thing and someone else seems to profit, we must keep focused on God's "big picture" and not become envious. The concept of "the big picture" is one that kept being repeated in Abram and Sarai's life. They got into trouble in Egypt because Sarai the sister meant safety for Abram; yet Sarai the wife would be the means of God providing salvation to the world. God kept telling Abram to remember "the big picture." The Creator and Sovereign Lord makes promises that are always delivered at just the right time.

Abram's nephew Lot and his people were enjoying the spoils of the land. He was camped on the outskirts of "sin city." Living on the edge of sin is dangerous and requires tremendous discipline to avoid slipping into bad situations and environments. Because of his physical proximity to the sinful cities, Lot got swept up into the political unrest of the communities. "The four kings seized all the goods of Sodom and Gomorrah and all their food; then went away. They also carried off Abram's nephew Lot and all his possessions, since he was living in Sodom" (Gen. 14:11-12).

In response to the attack on his extended family, Abram gathered 318 men and took on a leadership role to redeem the people that he believed God would use to build the promised nation. God took the human resources of Abram and multiplied their capabilities and allowed them to destroy the armies of four kings and ultimately rescue Lot. Melchizedek, the priest of God, blessed Abram. Then, Abram gave to God a tithe of 10% and swore His allegiance. Yet while his men were likely celebrating a victory and having a spiritual mountaintop experience, Abram was uneasy. Questions loomed in the back of his mind. Would there be retribution from the defeated parties? Plus he harbored the disappointment of ten more years and still no heir that God had promised.

Abram did not have a Bible to turn to for solace as we have, but God spoke directly to him, and His words were timely and encouraging, "I am your shield, your very great reward." God would be his protector and provision, and He consummated His covenant with Abram. It was a binding, one-sided contract that only required Abram's acknowledgement and acceptance. God promised to do all the heavy lifting. (You can read more about the covenant ceremony in Gen. 15:1–21). God continues to work the same way in our lives through Christ Jesus. His death on the cross provides a means for our salvation. His grace alone is enough, and we cannot earn God's favor. And it is with that point that we get to the heart of our focus on marriage, which begins in Genesis 16:1–16.

After the wars and spoils and success and riches, Abram and Sarai did not have a heart for earthly recognition. Instead, their life felt empty without children. Abram prayed, "O Sovereign Lord, what can you give me since I remain childless, and the one who will inherit my estate is Eliezer of Damascus…You have given me no children; so a servant in my household will be my heir" (Gen. 15:2-3). After the personal encounters with Jehovah, the couple's faith in Him had grown, but God's not meeting their timeframe for providing a child raised doubts in their minds about His promise. They probably began feeling like God's promised "product" was on "back order."

Do you ever have similar thoughts to those of Abram and Sarai? For example, you believe the Bible is true and that God did all those wonderful miracles. Your theology is sound, and you've been attending church as regularly as Abram built altars. You tithe like Abram, and you fight the good fight each day at work, at home, in school, and in the community. You have good days and bad days and faithfully believe that God will provide for your needs. But you have been praying about a situation, and instead of receiving delivery, you feel as though you've received God's "back-order" notice. The back order paperwork is always friendly in tone and reminds you that your business is appreciated, but the item you desire has not yet been shipped. Being a resourceful person, you strike out on your own to fix the problem. Fortunately, you live near Costco! They have everything at Costco, and you also can feed your camel for ten cents less a gallon than at the competition while you do your shopping. You try to look at the big picture as you carefully evaluate your decision tree options and prayer needs. Then you improvise and rationalize! God provided Costco, right? There couldn't be a Costco unless God provided the raw materials and brains to make it happen. Right?

So do you wait for God to take action, or do you take matters into your own hands? How long do you wait? Abram and Sarai were being taught that God was not interested in the timing in which He would answer their prayer; instead, He was interested in answering the prayer at the right time. That's a big difference. God's ultimate goal is to bring redemption and to be reconciled to all people through Jesus Christ. Abram and Sarai's son needed to be born at the right time so that Christ would arrive "…when the time had fully come…" (Galatians 4:4–5). Unfortunately, Abram and Sarai took matters into their own hands and metaphorically went to Costco for provision. They couldn't wait for the promise any longer and decided to fix things through their own means. Please understand that I am not suggesting that you simply sit on the sofa and do nothing, but I am saying that you should be more patient and prayerful than you have practiced being in the past. We have grown accustomed to "drive thru" service and begin thinking that God should respond in the same way. God works in and through His creation and people. He is not procrastinating; instead, He is purposefully providing for you at the right time.

After living forty years in a pagan land, Abram and Sarai had grown spiritually, but the on-going delay of having a baby created a painful time of testing. Sarai was barren, and no medical resources existed. A woman in this condition would feel hopeless and many times be treated as though she were to blame. The only way she would have a child would be through God's miraculous interaction. Yet God was not acting as quickly as they expected. He had promised that they would have offspring, but the biology and time had rendered her physically unable to conceive. So they decided to take matters into their own hands.

It was culturally acceptable to adopt a child or arrange one through a slave or maidservant surrogacy. After delivery of the child, the wife would be considered the mother and raise the baby as her own. The husband pledged financial responsibility and spousal privileges to the surrogate, and the baby would have full rights as an heir to the father's wealth. This solution is similar to what is practiced today. Women agree to artificial insemination and then promise to turn the child over for adoption at birth, while other women place their babies up for adoption. Surrogacy seemed to solve a long-term problem and immediately provided an answer to a prayer and desire for Abram and Sarai.

With that being said, let me add that what human hands try to provide will never equal God's promises. This statement doesn't mean that we should not pursue adoption. It is a godly provision, and it has been a blessing in our family. However, God had communicated specific plans for Abram and Sarai, but they got restless and pursued their own agenda. Were they prayerful, and did they ask God for direction? Based on the outcome of the story, we must assume that God was not a part of their decision. Instead, they selected a culturally acceptable practice in substitution for God's promised solution. Culturally-acceptable solutions are a part of our modern lives. A procedure or practice that is culturally acceptable or scientifically possible doesn't mean that it is God's plan for us or His best provision for our marriage.

The scope of this book is not to cover the medical aspects of infertility; although, solutions abound that are acceptable for Christians and others that should cause us to pause and pray. There is an old saying, "The days are slow, and the years are fast." What we feel we must accomplish today without God's direction may ease immediate stress and disappointment, but years of regret can follow. Regret is exactly what Abram and Sarai had to deal with after they selected Hagar as their surrogate mother. Abram had sexual relations with Hagar, and that intimacy, regardless of the practical intent, created a marital rift. As we have studied in the past, God intended for a couple to become one flesh both physically and spiritually. In God's eyes, Sarai had introduced and promoted a pagan practice of infidelity, and Abram went along with the custom. It was as though the table of integrity was now turned on Abram. Sarai asked Abram to go along with sin; whereas, he had requested that Sarai lie about their relationship in Egypt. Ironically, Sarai felt betrayed by her husband. Hagar had taken the role of carrying Abram's future heir and was no longer just a slave. Her child would be Abram's seed for a nation. She was carrying the baby and doing all the work, and it would be human nature for her to be prideful in her accomplishment and new social status. It is unlikely that Hagar sold herself into slavery. Instead, she was likely a gift from the Egyptian Pharaoh (see Gen. 12:16). The pregnancy moved her from the role of slave to an honored member of the family. But as much as the result could have pleased Hagar, it irked Sarai. One surmises that every time Abram glanced at Hagar to inquire about the wellbeing of the baby, it reminded Sarai of what she could not provide. Nine months of tension and envy conflicted with the excitement of the baby's arrival.

Aspects of that situation can play out in the lives of modern Christians. Many times I have seen couples in our young married Sunday school class transform from honeymooners into parents. During the excitement of baby announcements, there are always a few couples remaining that are unable to or delayed in becoming pregnant as quickly as they desire. Joyous moments also hold a painful reminder of a current childless condition. Time in these instances does not "heal all wounds," and that is where our application meshes with the Bible account.

Time and disappointment had been eating away at Sarai and Abram for years. Now for nine months, the threefold cord of husband, wife, and God had gained another member. It was an uncomfortable, crowded, and unhealthy marriage environment. It is unlikely that Abram loved Hagar or was romantically predisposed to her. Certainly Hagar was important to him because she carried his child. In Abram's mind, Hagar's child was the promise of God. But Abram took a hands-off approach to the strife between Sarai and Hagar. Hands-off would have been the smart decision when Sarai came to him with the idea, but now the consequences of sin would play out in all their lives! Jealously took root, and it seems that the stress impacted the family and community relationships. People in the encampment most likely had to walk "on eggshells" when they worked around Abram, Sarai, and Hagar. Then, bad matters only got worse. Sarai treated Hagar harshly, which may translate into Hagar returning to the role of slave or being treated with jealous distain instead of appreciation. Family life was a mess and looked like a modern-day reality TV show!

Hagar could no longer tolerate the abuse. She gathered herself up and hastily departed the camp. How quickly sin will damage relationships! Sin can be forgiven, but the consequences can be long-lasting and painful. Living apart from God's guiding hand was now destroying the very possession that enticed Abram and Sarai to sin! The child they desired was now on the way to Egypt with his distraught birth mother.

What are some of the relational mistakes that you should identify and avoid in your marriage? Sarai had the idea to use Hagar instead waiting for God's promise. She misused her role as a godly helper to Abram, much like Eve did in the Adam and Eve story. Sin begins when the husband and wife roles are ignored or confused. Then guilt and blame begin to harm the relationship. Abram agreed with Sarai's plan, and yet she felt Abram had betrayed her. She blamed Abram, saying, "You are responsible for the wrong I am suffering…" (Gen. 16:5). Abram responded in defeat instead of leadership. He essentially replied that it was Sarai's fault for creating the situation, and she should manage the "domestic problem" as she desired. Abram and Sarai were at odds with one another and with God. Hagar was disillusioned, and an innocent baby was in the desert. In modern families, this amount of tension, sin, and unhappiness could place a family on the road to divorce. God does not want these kinds of relationships for His children.

People often treat God as though His rules are harsh and limiting. Instead, healthy relationship boundaries are His gift. God did not storm into the situation and punish, but the consequences inflicted a self-punishment. Just like Abram and Sarai had to, families must deal with the circumstances of sin. The Bible shows God's mercy and loving-kindness is available even when we fail. God never stops loving us! He is always seeking to redeem His creation and reestablish or maintain a relationship. He never will give up on you or your marriage, no matter how difficult the circumstances or complicated the sin. He never gave up on Abram and Sarai, and they gave Him plenty of reasons to become frustrated.

Regardless of century, people are born hard-wired to do right and moral things, but when they stray from God's circuit board, trouble occurs. God loves us enough to allow us choices, even bad choices. But God is equally desirous of our turning to Him for help as His people. Hagar was hurting and heading down a pathway that would take her back home to Egypt, and God was with her all the way. He ministered to her, sent her divine help, and explained that her son's offspring would become a great nation. But the animosity between Sarai and Hagar would be passed down through the generations. The emotional baggage created and carried by Sarai and Hagar would be learned by their offspring. Generations of people pick up the baggage left behind by family and friends. You should ask yourself, "Is there emotional baggage that my parents have handed me that I continue to carry into my marriage and will hand to my children one day?" There is no better time to start traveling lighter than right now!

God illustrated that He loved both Hagar and the child. He promised that she would become a matriarch and her son would become the father of a great tribe living in the desert. However, they were not His promised nation. Hagar's child bore the Arab nation. It has been a nemesis to Israel for many generations. Additionally, Sarai's great, great grandson Joseph would one day be captured and taken to Egypt by Ishmael's offspring, but God's plan would prevail!

God has a specific plan for your life. You are not drifting aimlessly. Sarai and Abram may have felt at times like their life was drifting or like they were victims of chance, but we can see in retrospect that their life was no accident. God had a plan for them. They often took unnecessary detours, but He had a plan nonetheless. Some days they looked at God's provision as a gift and other times as a curse.

How about you? Do you view the circumstances that don't meet your expectations as God not caring about your needs? You can gain confidence in God through His Bible message! He is intentional and specific about your journey. Each couple's waypoints are different, but God's desire for your destination is identical. He wants you to trust Him and enjoy Him forever in His heavenly home. Our challenge is in trusting and embracing the journey, even when we are disappointed with the typography of our path. We sometimes get a little envious, and then that leads to our trying to fix things ourselves. I am pretty handy at fixing broken things, but I continually make mistakes when I try to fix people and situations. Fixing people is God's work. My best work seems to be mending Barbie Doll heads, rotating tires, and honoring God by loving my family.

The Hagar episode in Abram and Sarai's life ended well. The baby was born and named Ishmael, just as the angel in the desert had instructed Hagar. Ishmael means "One who hears." Although Hagar was raised in a pagan nation, God loved her and sent an angel to comfort and communicate His promise to her. God heard her plea. If God heard the plea of an Egyptian slave girl, then it is logical to believe that He hadn't forgotten His promise to bless Abram and Sarai. Of course, we have the luxury of looking at their journey with 20/20 hindsight. Their lack of faith in God led them to the wrong conclusion. This was followed by sin, regret, and a life of uncomfortable consequences.

Sometimes we allow the daily grind to wear us down and make us believe that God will not help or deliver us. But God doesn't work on a timetable that is based upon our reaching retirement at the right age, location, and appropriate savings account balance. Forty to fifty years had passed since Abram and Sarai left home. Now that Ishmael was born, for the next thirteen years they would continue to assume that he was the promised one. But as I mentioned earlier, barren land does not mean worthless! Barren can mean not ready. The journey that Abram and Sarai were traveling was God's intentional way of preparing them for a gift that would be delivered, and it would be a blessing to generations.

. . . .

CHAPTER 9

Growth through Detours

Y OU MAY HAVE heard the concept, "Pray like everything is up to God, but work like everything is up to you." I don't know who coined the phrase, but the idea is that we rely upon God and that in doing so, we allow ourselves to be His instruments. But there is a tension that exists between doing and being that requires an intentional effort on our part to commune with God so that we properly apply the concept. It is easy to get off track if we do not actively verify our position in Christ.

When you are navigating a boat, drift can be your worst enemy. Unlike when you are driving an automobile or walking on a sidewalk, when you are piloting a boat, water traffic lanes are not clearly identifiable. Even in the inner coastal waterway, where navigational aids mark the safely-navigable ditch of water, a boater must constantly be aware of the catalysts of drift. Current, wind, and tide can hamper, enhance, or impede your course. Therefore the skipper must monitor the GPS, charts, compass, and navigational aids so that he does not run aground and damage his vessel or create collateral damage. It is challenging and sometimes frightening, but it also can be fun if you know what you are doing and can keep your wits about you when moments of stress arrive.

How about you? How are you positioned with God? Have you checked with Him through prayer and patiently sought His answers?

As we follow along the journey of Abram and Sarai, we see a couple that faced the challenge of marriage in a pagan world. They were challenged with the journey that God had chosen for them. We have seen some of their frustrations and fright, and we can apply some of the aspects of their marriage to ours. For example, we can recognize that God allows His people to encounter a fallen world, and through that experience, they have a choice to trust God or seek their own solutions. The Christian walk does not mean we will not have to work to succeed, deal with difficult family members, or encounter troublemaking neighbors. God does not grab the tiller and steer us *around* difficult circumstances. Instead, we must navigate *through* the storm. With His help, the journey can be so much more productive and rewarding. God doesn't simply want you to *get* through a troubling circumstance. He wants you to *grow* through the trouble. It is that growth that prepares you for His service. It was the growth through trials and trouble that challenged Sarai and Abram and made them ready to move from barren to fruitful for God.

Abram was a strong man physically and mentally. He was willing to fight the good fight, but encounters with authority would sometimes sap his energy. Abram loved life, and he was a born survivor. He could fix things because he was resourceful. When he was resourceful with God, he could defeat the armies of four kings. When he was resourceful alone, he would find himself in jeopardy of losing the one

God provided to give birth to an heir. Abram and Sarai had taken God's promise of a child into their own hands. Their actions created a legal heir through the handmaid Hagar. Although that practice of overcoming infertility was culturally acceptable, it was not godly. Ishmael was a fleshly product of unfaithfulness instead of the spiritual promise from God. Sarai and Abram were unfaithful to each other and unfaithful to God. Their sin impacted Hagar and generations of people who have been challenged to live peacefully with the descendants of Ishmael.

In Sarai and Abram's eyes, God was not sufficient to meet all their needs. He was God, but with a little "g." That attitude is not too different from how Christians think of God and worship Him today. Many people believe that God is a distant energy source who is permissive of all cultural practices and religions and is manipulated by good deeds or positive thinking. Although He is not worshiped as Creator, unbelievers blame Him for earthly disasters or unrealized plans and dreams. Inversely, there those who live their lives clinging to the hope that God doesn't exist and spend their time and resources on a self-medicated meaning of life that ends in loneliness or futility. So often this poor way of thinking is the fruit of sin or discouraging circumstances.

Thirteen years is a long time to wait for God—even thirteen days can seem like forever. But then God again appeared before Abram and stated that He is El Shaddai. That name is translated "God Almighty." The name also meant "The Mountain One." Mountains were seen as powerful, as stable, and as obstacles. Therefore, God spoke to Abram as the One who rules over the obstacles! In Isaiah 40:4, it is written that when God's redemption is complete, "...every mountain and hill will be made low." And in the gospel of Mark (11:23) Jesus states, " I tell you the truth, if anyone says to this mountain, 'Go, throw yourself into the sea' and does not doubt in his heart but believes that what he says will happen, it will be *done* for him." (emphasis mine).

Abram and Sarai had doubts along the way, and they rejected the concept that God would rule over the obstacle of infertility. So God stated in Genesis 17:1, "...walk before Me, and be blameless." Abram had made the mistake of walking before Sarai and not God. Abram had agreed to do the wrong thing, and then she blamed him for the relationship problems. God told Abram that he was to walk before Him, do the right thing, and trust Him. The Air Force used to have a motto: "Aim High." The phrase brought together the concept of flight and excellence. God was encouraging Abram to "Aim High" at pleasing Him, or to be blameless.

Please understand that this command does not mean perfection because we will not achieve perfection until we are united with God. But it does mean that we are not to make our walk fit our imperfections. For example, a teacher's goal is not for everyone to learn to read like the weakest reader in the class; the teacher wants each student to excel and become a better reader. That concept rings true in sports, business, and marriage. We are to walk with a sincere intent and constant desire for holiness. We do this because we love our heavenly Father and, in turn, want to love our spouse properly.

Abram's response to God's voice was to fall flat, face down, spiritually convicted that he had fallen far short of God's desire for his life. The best of men are men at best, and that described Abram. He often fell short of having godly faith, and he would fall short again. God did not select Abram for what he could do for Him, but for what God could do through Abram. God again and again told Abram of the obstacles He would remove from Abram's life and of His divine intervention. Through the lives of Abram and Sarai, God would transform the world!

This family's transformation began with a name change. As I mentioned before, in the ancient Middle East, a man or woman's name was not predictive of the person he or she would become, but it was intended to be prescriptive. Abram's name meant "exalted father," but the name Abraham meant "father of a multitude." His new name was a forecast of the man God would make of him. I can imagine the smirks that Abraham received when he told the guys back at the encampment to call him Abraham and his wife was now to be called Sarah. She went from being called "princess" to "one who will produce kings." The names likely rang a little hollow with his employees, but it did not ring hollow with Abraham.

When God said Sarah would have a child, Abraham fell down, laughing with astonishment, and Sarah giggled behind the tent door. The concept of a 100-year-old man and ninety-year-old woman having children was preposterous and entertaining. It was one of those moments when faith and experience met at the crossroad of life. In essence, they were emotionally overwhelmed when they considered the possibility and a bit embarrassed as they hoped it would come true. It is risky to share with others the kind of faith that believes regardless of worldly circumstances that seem impossible. Satan will tempt you, saying that it is wishful thinking, and the world will anticipate and celebrate your downfall. But our loving and merciful God replied to Abraham and Sarah (paraphrased), "Laugh if you will. In fact, you and Sarah will name the baby laughter," which was translated Isaac! Once again, God responded in love! It is the kind of love that you must display when your spouse won't believe you or rejects your testimony. God then proceeded to explain the "big picture" and the impact that their marriage would have upon the world. He also addressed the mistaken identity of Ishmael and promised to take care of that child in a specific way. He also clarified that Ishmael would not inherit the covenant promised through Isaac.

There is an old hymn that goes, "Nothing is Impossible if you put your trust in God." God would make the impossible promise a reality through an ancient relationship called a Suzerain-Vassal treaty. That kind of agreement stated that the King (God) was responsible for fulfillment of the decree. The Vassal (Abraham) was a powerless follower and agreed to the contract's stipulations. He had no input to the terms of the agreement, but he would be blessed if he followed the contract and cursed if he rejected the contract guidelines. This is similar to the New Testament concept of grace. Jesus' death on the cross to pay the price for our sins was an act of grace. It was an act performed on our behalf to reconcile us to our holy Father, but we do not deserve grace, nor do we earn grace. Believers/followers of Jesus are simply acceptors of the gift of grace. Our discipleship is rewarded by eternal life, and our rejection results in eternal banishment.

The agreement with Abraham would be consummated through the mysterious act of circumcision. I have heard this term in church all my life and understand the medical procedure, but it is seldom explained because of polite decorum. We all know what happens, but we don't say much about it because it is rather private. When discussing this, we must first remember that God did not create sex to be dirty. Humans have done that for Him. Second, we must remember that the situation is not sexual because circumcision is done on babies. It was to be a private affair for the family and priest.

Circumcision is the removal of a portion of flesh. Metaphorically, flesh was considered evil. Abraham and

Sarah had made fleshly plans in how they gained an heir through Ishmael. Their fleshly way of plotting and scheming continually got them into trouble. So circumcision would be a one-time removal and a reminder of the removal of fleshly plans. It was also a visual reminder for those who would fall in and under the community of Abraham. The community of Abraham would become the community or nation of God. It would be from that nation that God's Son, Jesus, would be born.

Circumcision has become commonplace in America, and generally, it is no longer a religious rite. Christians often quote the apostle Paul's phrase "circumcision of the heart," which focuses on removing the worldly way of living and replacing it with life in the spirit. The New Testament has replaced the rite of circumcision with baptism. Where circumcision is the removal of a portion of evil flesh, baptism is the death of evil flesh. When you are baptized in a pool of water, you are metaphorically dead, buried, and then raised with Christ. The intent is to put the fleshly way of living to death. The baptism itself is nothing more than water and symbolism. Nothing in the water purifies anymore than the flint knife purified Abraham or his family.

Abraham and Sarah had focused too much of their confidence in the flesh instead of God. Paul writes in Philippians 3:3, "For it is we who are the circumcision, we who worship in the Spirit of God, who glory in Christ Jesus, and put no confidence in the flesh..." God did not want the patriarch of the nation of Israel to follow a confidence in the flesh. Therefore, all men in that nation were to submit to the rite as a reminder of who they were in the family of God. Abraham wasn't simply able to say, "I get it," and move on in the agreement with God. Instead, God required that he use a knife and experience the pain and the constant visual reminder of the event. It was a one-time event that would reflect an eternal commitment, just as God's promises were permanent and eternal.

We see a parallel to this in the one-time repentance and belief in Christ that brings about our salvation. We, too, have those kinds of commitments in our faith journey. Baptism is an outward sign or rite to an internal commitment. Baptism is a rite that God places in our path that allows us to illustrate a visual act of loyalty that represents an internal commitment to follow Christ.

Our marriage covenant with our spouse is also a commitment with God. We go through a great deal of effort and expense for the ceremony. That is a rite that isn't required for marriage. We simply can go to the courthouse, file the proper papers, and away we go. But humans have an innate desire to perform a rite. Those desires are a reflection of the ancient times, when men like Abraham built an altar to worship God or stacked stones as a sign or memorial that illustrated their relationship with God to the world. Even pagan nations and tribes have rites. Therefore, it is reasonable to believe that it is a God-given desire in man to identify himself with something greater than himself. Those very practices point to a Creator that has made man in His image. Man is creative, but he cannot be more creative than the One who created him. Therefore, regardless of the depravity and fallen nature of man, God's image still surfaces through man's need to perform a rite. Therefore, man's commitments are both visual and verbal; although, pagan rituals are meaningless if they are not focused upon the one true, living, and eternal God.

Can you see how God's fingerprints in creation continue to witness about Him? Do you realize why your lasting marriage covenant is also God's witness to an unbelieving world?

Abraham immediately obeyed God, without negotiating or whining. The Scripture states, "That very day," he faithfully obeyed God and took that commitment back to the camp. Everyone in Abraham's household submitted to God. If you think that trying to convince people to call you by a new name is difficult, then try and tell a community of men and boys that it is circumcision time around the campfire! "And every male in Abraham's household, including those born in his household or bought from a foreigner was circumcised with him" (Gen. 17:27).

The commitment to God was not casual. It was not a theological bumper sticker or fodder for political debate and misuse. It was painful, required a knife and blood, and resulted in a lifetime sign and commitment. I believe it was also God's way of allowing Abraham and the nation of Israel to have some "skin in the game." Today it is only used for health reasons, but then it signified a life-changing action, response, and commitment to follow God.

The marriage commitment to our spouse and with God should not be casual. Those who live together in a committed relationship but have not committed to marriage as God desires are living in sin. How often have you heard someone say, "It is only a piece of paper, and we don't need a piece of paper to be committed to marriage"? That comment is wrong and illustrates an affront to God because it indicates an unwillingness to submit to God and cherish His gift of marriage.

Today, marriage has become too much of a negotiated contract that has loopholes and exit strategies. God did not bless your marriage until the warranty runs out. There is no middle ground in following God. In reviewing the covenant with Abraham, I cannot find middle ground in God's promises or what He expected. Abraham performed a rite of separation from his old life started a new life with a new name. (In Ur of the Chaldeans, they did not practice circumcision or worship God.) Abraham and Sarah committed themselves, their family, and their household to the worship of the one, true God. Their marriage was and yours is to be a life-changing promise to one another and to God.

What one thing in your marriage do you need to "circumcise" and then commit to God and to one another? Is there a spiritual Ishmael in your life that you keep asking God to bless, and God keeps denying your request? Is there an issue of a religious rite that you know in the back of your mind and heart that God is calling you to address? Abraham made a lot of mistakes in his life, but when God told him to do something, he did not waste any time. He made things happen! What do you need to make happen today so that you can walk blamelessly before God?

If those questions get the attention of your heart, then talk to your spouse about your concerns. Then both you and your spouse take it to God in prayer. Those are the kinds of prayers God answers!

CHAPTER 10

. . . .

Finishing Strong

E IGHT YEARS AGO, Terry and I began a kitchen re-modeling project. We found an excellent contractor, and to this day, we count him as a good friend. We also continue to enjoy the investment. I vividly remember the day that the contractor came to tell me that we would have to demolish a portion of the house instead of using it as a foundation for the new construction. I had recently had the house reroofed, which was a worthy but not enjoyable expense. His suggestion required removing 30% of the brand-new roof and putting it in a dumpster. I originally had expected to begin expanding upon the existing footprint, but that plan would mean spending money on demolition and construction. I protested, "Why shouldn't we use the existing foundation, roof, and walls for the expansion?" My idea seemed to make logical sense.

My contractor replied, "It isn't that you cannot use the existing portion of the house for your construction, but you shouldn't. The walls, ceiling, and floor are not level or square; therefore, everything added to that space will need to be built crooked. Your doors, molding, and kitchen cabinets will never fit properly. I'll do what you think is best, but my recommendation is that you start with a proper foundation before you expand your home. You won't save money by using the existing structure because it will take more labor to build everything to fit a crooked space. You may never enjoy the results if you don't allow me to tear down the existing and build with new material and with strict quality specifications."

I relented, and a man climbed on the roof with a saw and cut from gutter to gutter to remove the roof. I had to go lie down to get over the shock!

The moral of the story: Before you can finish strong, you have to start strong. A building must have the correct foundation or everything you add to it will be flawed. That basic truth in carpentry also applies to business, governments, and marriages. You cannot build a strong marriage upon a poor foundation. It will last for a while, but as you add additional materials, the structure will continue to weaken. Then the test of the structure occurs during a storm. When the rains come, you do not want to start patching the roof or digging trenches to drain water from the foundation.

So how does this illustration pertain to Abraham and Sarah? God began building in them a foundation of godliness the moment they began their journey away from Ur of the Chaldeans. Their walk of faith was progressive in God's eyes and to those in their community. Their accomplishment of growing in faith wasn't measured by personal achievement, but instead, it was measured by their willingness to allow God to work through them. When they relied upon their resourcefulness, they failed and were in need of God's divine delivery.

Until a short time ago, I have been guilty of resenting the fact that government inspectors were overseeing our recent bedroom remodeling project. It was my opinion that their intrusion retarded the project and provided no value. This I believed until I had to fire the contractor and begin to complete the project myself. Overnight I became the general contractor.

When a home is being built, the inspector comes to the site to insure that the structure meets the minimum requirements for soundness. Any one building infraction in and of itself may be insignificant. But the end result requires a sound foundation and proper building material. Therefore, the evaluation by the inspector becomes a welcome confirmation to the homeowner/contractor. The time to find deficiencies in plumbing is not when you are taking a shower. Just as the time to find mistakes in the electric wiring is not when you are in the dark and the walls are closed up tightly, painted, and adorned with art.

The inspection process and the results are of little lasting value to the inspector. He knows where to look, knows the necessary specifications, and foresees the end results. Instead the inspection benefits the homeowner as it allows him to validate the quality in each step of the project. Without an inspector, he becomes too focused on eliminating trips to Home Depot, retarding the financial drain, and exorcising the constant stream of hard-hat-adorned strangers into his home. The homeowner simply desires the destination of a good night's sleep in the new bedroom that has been under construction for so long and cost him more money and stress than he imagined when the plans initially were drawn. God's plan is not simply that we go to heaven when we die, but that we continue to grow in faith and discipleship in Christ Jesus each step of the way. Colossians 3:10-11 states, "...put on the new self who is being renewed to a true knowledge according to the image of the One who created Him."

In chapter 22 of Genesis, we read of Abraham's final test or in building terms: a godly inspection. The test is not for God's sake, because He foresees the outcome. God is not anxiously anticipating Abraham's step before He can make a decision, nor is God delayed or discouraged by the building process. Instead, His role is that of the inspector who helps the couple discover deficiencies in their spiritual construction and, in turn, will direct them to make the required changes to insure safety and soundness.

As we close in on the final construction punch list of Abraham and Sarah's godly marriage, we will review the time in their life after Sodom and Gomorrah have been destroyed. Here are some of the things that happened: Lot's family felt a crushing blow as his wife, likely raised in one of those sinful communities, fell victim to the deception of the world. Abraham and Sarah encountered another king who wanted Sarah for his harem. And again they lied and told him she was only a sister to Abraham! Laughter and joy entered the home of Abraham and Sarah in the form of Isaac. (His name was a reflection of both Abraham and Sarah's responses to God's promise and their initial reactions to God's promise of a baby.) And then the three-way-parenting trap that had disrupted their home life had been eliminated with the departure of Hagar and Ishmael.

Remember our discussion on sin and baggage? Based on their reaction to the king, it looks like Abraham and Sarah continued to carry the baggage of fear during that time. It seems that God allows us to encounter the same challenging weaknesses again and again until we trust Him! Are you having a similar experience in your marriage? Remember, it is easier to travel light and let God do the heavy lifting.

Satan's temptation and Adam and Eve's rejection of God's code for living brought about a curse on the world, and it has impacted the marriage relationship ever since. That curse separated man from a relationship with God. God, since He is holy and just, cannot accept projects that ignore the basic elements of safe and sound living. Yet God does not simply give up on His creation; instead, He comes to interact with it. When I had to fire my contractor, one of the first calls I made was to the building inspector. "I'm in trouble," I stated, "and I need someone to help me through this process."

The inspector did not pull out the rulebook and begin counting nails. He replied, "Mr. Akins, you are not in trouble. I have good news for you!"

After Abram and Sarai's mistakes, God did not rain fire upon them. Granted, they had to deal with the cost of the situation, just as I have had to pay the cost for repairing problems and purchasing new materials. The consequences of sin are real, and we must deal with them. However, God did not come to read from the codebook of life; He brought the good news of eternal life! And God initially brought that good news through the gift of marriage! He looked down at all the construction and destruction going on in the world and chose Abraham and Sarah as the family that would build a marriage, family, and a nation of God. Through them, God would deliver to the world a Savior.

Abraham and Sarah now had everything they ever wanted. They had a fruitful life, financial prosperity, a son, and grandchildren to anticipate. The building of God's nation and the reconciliation of creation were advancing toward a "silent night, a holy night," when a child of promise would deliver the world from sin and death. But was the family foundation built by Abraham and Sarah ready to support God's plan and withstand the test of time and the elements?

God's test for Abraham and Sarah would be radical, and most people would agree that God's request seemed ridiculous. God would ask Abraham to sacrifice Isaac upon the altar, like an animal! The idea seemed ungodly because pagans practiced child sacrifice. It reminds me of my home inspector coming out to the construction site and saying that I needed hurricane clips added to the roof. "That request is crazy," I replied. "We live in Atlanta, not Florida, and we don't have hurricanes." But for about $2 per clip, I was able to prepare our home and further protect us against difficult weather conditions. What God asks us to do isn't always about the task we are to complete; it is often about our willingness to obey Him. God didn't want Abraham to sacrifice Isaac. God was teaching Abraham how to finish strong!

I bet Abraham thought his best days were behind him and that he was prepared to retire in "Sunny Valley" for the last act. (Since I have been married now for twenty-five years, this part of the story gives me great encouragement because I trust God still has things for us to do in His name!) Abraham and his family were living peacefully in the land of the Philistines. It was a time of worshiping the "Everlasting God," who had grown and prospered Abraham. Much of God's promise had been delivered, and Abraham had fulfilled his commitment to God. But there was a long-range element of the promise, the prophecy of the "seed" that was not yet delivered. That "seed" would be Jesus, and through Him, the world would be delivered from sin and death. Just as God declared Abraham righteous because of his faith, all men would have the opportunity to be declared righteous through their faith in Christ Jesus.

Already God's spoken words to Abraham sounded like a line from the New Testament when He described Isaac as his "only begotten son" and "the son you love." Those descriptors foreshadow God's description of His Son, Jesus. You may be thinking that Abraham had more than one son, as Ishmael was born of Hagar through Abraham. True, but the son of God's promise was Isaac. He was the one that they had desired and strived to produce on their own. But just as man strives to create his own salvation through cults, good deeds, religion, and spiritual practices, salvation cannot be accomplished through man's activities. Only God, the Creator, can provide salvation to those who accept His only begotten Son, Jesus Christ. This portion of the story sheds light on what it means for parents to sacrifice as God the Father sacrificed for us.

So Abraham received his instructions and got up early in the morning to begin the journey with Isaac. Although Abraham did not know how God's request would play out, he did not delay in responding. He was to take Isaac to a place God would show him along the way and offer him back to God as a sacrifice. That kind of sacrifice was specific and certainly not metaphorical. God specified that Isaac was to be a burnt offering. The sacrifice would not be a gesture or sign; Isaac would be totally destroyed.

This makes me think of how we read of religious groups today that believe that Jesus swooned or was only spiritually crucified on the cross. That kind of thinking is not intellectually logical. The Romans were masters at punishing people to death, and they did not make any mistakes with Jesus.

The Bible does not mention how Sarah was dealing with this situation, only that Abraham, as God's assigned head of the household, faithfully followed God's instructions. The description of this historic event reflects God's plan for headship of the family. Ultimately, the nation of Israel would be built upon Abraham's shoulders. His responsibilities required submission and trust in God and illustrated how a husband is to lead his family. He is to be a servant to God first and then accountable to God when leading his family. I recognize that our society rebels against male leadership in the home. But why wouldn't a wife desire this kind of godly leader for a husband? He is a man first responsible to his Creator and then lovingly applying God's loving-kindness in the home.

Abraham was told to travel to the region of Moriah. It is a rocky area outside of the future city of Jerusalem and possibly on the site that King David proposed the construction of the temple. The trip would take three days and require supplies and helpers. Genesis 21:11 describes Abraham's frame of mind, "Abraham was greatly distressed." Some commentators note that the recording of Abraham's preparation seems a bit out of order. For example, he saddled the donkey, called everyone together, and then started cutting firewood. Typically, a person would first call everyone together, collect supplies, and then saddle and load the animals. God's Word is specific and purposeful. Therefore, the out-of-sequence description seems to indicate a person who is stressed but working through his stress in order to follow God's directions. What a wonderful model for contemporary Christians to follow! It is likely that he was being pelted with mental temptations to avoid the situation, slowdown, and presume that God was wrong. But Abraham carried on and planted one foot in front of the other.

During the three-day sojourn, Abraham kept any doubt to himself and only spoke with godly confidence. I can only image the dread as Abraham "looked up" to the high place and knew that His next steps would be the most difficult. Hebrews 11:17–19 indicates that Abraham spoke to the servants with undying faith that somehow this difficult task would be accomplished as God desired. Of all the times he had failed God, God had never failed Abraham and Sarah! This day, His fears were overcome by faith! Abraham believed that God's promise would be fulfilled through Isaac in some miraculous way.

Like Abraham, you may not know all the answers, but you know Jesus, our God, and can trust Him. Abraham faithfully followed God regardless of the temptations of a dizzying circumstance. He put the wood for the fire on his son's back, an event that provides another prophetic moment as God allowed Jesus, His only begotten Son, to have wood upon his back as they nailed Him to the cross. Then Abraham carried the torch or the "fire" as described in the Bible. He arrived with a lit torch. We can wonder in our mind's eye if Sarah saw that flickering flame as she watched Abraham depart three days earlier.

Abraham carried the flame of hope. He held tightly to the flame of God's love and promise. Isaac was old enough to carry wood, and along the steep trail, he asked his father why they did not have a sacrificial lamb. Abraham's response reflected a man whose walk was totally devoted to faith and trust in God. He answered with a truth that every married couple can cling to in times of uncertainty, "God Himself will provide!"

If Isaac was large enough to carry the wood, he also was large enough to flee his elderly father. Yet Scripture states that Abraham laid him upon the stone altar and wood. There was no struggle, and Flavius Josephus, a Roman Historian of the first century, explained that Isaac was a godly son, who willingly submitted himself to the sacrifice. Isaac's submissive response speaks to the home life that Sarah and Abraham provided. He was the offspring of two people of godly discipleship.

Nothing stood in the way of Abraham's duty, and he drew the knife. The crude weapon of hammered metal was honed sharp for death and destruction. Abraham raised it above his head and swiftly began its plunge into the heart of Isaac. It was at that moment, the moment of fateful commitment, that an angel of God seized Abraham's arm and prevented him from stabbing Isaac.

God's voice then filled the air, "Now I know that you fear God, because you have not withheld from me your son, your only son." (Gen. 22:12). God was not saying that He was surprised at Abraham's decision, because God foresaw the event. "To know" someone as in this terminology reflects a relational intimacy of two persons experiencing something together. Both God and Abraham knew each other in the same way that a man and woman are to live as "one flesh." Their relationship was intimate and in one accord. God's will was reflected back to Him from the heart of Abraham. Abraham was fully committed to Him, beyond all the things he held dear.

Is that not the kind of relationship that you desired when you told the minister "I do" on your wedding day? A commitment of that magnitude must take deep root in the rich "relationship soil" with God before it can grow and blossom with your spouse.

After God spoke, Abraham once again lifted his eyes for God's provision and saw that a ram was tangled in the undergrowth of a nearby thicket. It was the sacrifice that Isaac had inquired about as they ascended the mountain. The ram was the substitution for Isaac that God provided for Abraham.

Once again, this interaction with Abraham pointed to God's Son, who would be born from the family of Abraham and be the substitution for the sin of the world. Jesus took man's position on the cross as an innocent and sinless substitution so that man would not have to die for his sins. As John 3:16–17 says (paraphrase mine), For God so loved

the world (we can put your names in place of "world") that
He gave His only begotten Son that all who place their faith
in Him shall not die (be eternally separated from God) but,
instead, they shall have life eternally with God. For God
did not send His Son into the world to condemn it for sin
but to save it from sin.

So how do you apply this dramatic event on the rock
outcropping near present day Jerusalem? First, we know that
God never intended for Isaac to die. God had the scenario
fully planned: the place, the moment, the angel, and the ram.
So was God treating Abraham like a puppet on a string?
No, God gives each of us a choice to accept or reject Him.
Abraham trusted God fully; it was a trust beyond intellectual
belief or a passing moment of emotional sentimentalism. It
was a trust based on a life lived for God and in the face of
many scenarios that often made no sense to neighbors who
did not know God. Hebrews 9:17 states, "Abraham reasoned
that God could raise the dead, and figuratively speaking, he
did receive Isaac back from death."

Can you imagine what it would be like to live with a
spouse who trusted God's provision at the level Abraham did
and who loved and trusted you the same way? Is it not the
destination that we all hope for and dream about as we meet
our beloved at God's altar? A husband who loved God in
that manner would be like a knight in shining armor. A wife
who loved God to that level would bring joy and fulfillment
to a man's heart and mind. Are you that kind of person to
your spouse? Do you want to be? The solution rests first
in first making God that inseparable person in your heart.
He brings hope, promise, forgiveness, love, encouragement,
joy, support, and truth into the lives of those who embrace
Him. You can only give away what you first have been given!
It is therefore through God that you can achieve a godly
marriage, the marriage that He desires for you.

We have been reading about Abraham's challenges of love for and commitment to Sarah. Fear and the lack of faith in God led to sinful mistakes, and it resonated in their marriage. Circumstances tested them, and many times he and his wife failed, but God never gave up on them. In turn, Abraham learned never to give up on His relationship with God. Abraham's actions illustrated that he would not allow anything to come between him and his love for God. He was a changed man; he was a godly leader of his family, devoted father, and husband. Abraham was the kind of man who God can use to bless everyone who reads His story and believes.

And so our journey with Abraham and Sarah ends with them living, loving, and learning in the region of Beersheba. The story of Abraham and Sarah provides God's timeless truths that you can apply to strengthen your marriage. I hope that you will continue to ponder the story, reread the biblical account, and ask God to reveal relevant applications for your marriage. You can rest assured that God will not call you to sacrifice your children as he asked Abraham to, but there will be times of sacrifice, challenge, and blessings. God skillfully crafts your marriage journey, and the way you apply His truths provides you with a way of worshiping God. Isn't that what God was trying to teach Abraham and Sarah during their journey? Just like the old hymn that we often sing in church, Abraham and Sarah learned to "trust and obey for there's no better way...."

Conclusion

I WANT TO review a few applications from *Travels with Abraham and Sarah* and challenge you to pray for God's continued revelation for your three-fold cord of marriage.

God's leadership is intentional. He is not a God of circumstances, happenstance, or karma. God shows us that there is to be a hierarchy in the family. Man is in the spiritual leadership role and is held to godly accountability. The woman is an equal helpmate in seeking God's direction and helping her husband make holy decisions. In all cases, God must remain at the pinnacle of your marriage. It is a divine chain of command or organization chart that has the purpose of protecting you and helping you to grow to be His holy witness to a lost world.

God is "El Shaddai," the mighty mountain and the One who will help you overcome all obstacles.

God provides what is needed at the moment it is most needed. God did not send the ram to Isaac and Abraham during the three-day journey. He did not answer Abraham's prayer during their mountain assent or when the knife was unsheathed. The ram was provided at the moment it was most needed. Yes, that kind of relationship will test your strength, courage, and faith, but you cannot grow without exercise. You are God's glorious creation, and as Christians, you are His sons and daughters through Christ Jesus. God does not provide for His family on their terms, but in His perfect timing.

When God's command becomes clear, you are to act. Abraham did not stand around pondering once he knew God's will. He acted immediately and decisively. Following God's way may not always make sense. Instead, God's way may cause discomfort and stress and require you to overcome conventional worldly wisdom. It can be heartbreaking, and initially, it can sap your strength. But God's way requires you to "look up" for God's help, just as Abraham looked up and saw the provision of a ram.

God must be your foremost focus and desire. Christians often say that God and their families are most important, followed by work, health, financial concerns, and other things. Many of us fall far short in applying that honorable phrase. God told Abraham to walk before Him and be blameless. At times, Abraham had walked before Sarah and had made some unwise decisions and cast blame. He so desired a child that once Isaac arrived, Abraham's neighbors may have thought he was walking before Isaac. I see many young married people move from a godly focus to a child focus when their baby arrives. Their time, resources, and finances turn inward and away from God and being a Christian witness. The development and provision for the family is highly important, but Abraham's biggest test came after the promise of a son was delivered. Abraham modeled that pleasing God was of paramount importance to him. You cannot properly love your spouse or children until you know how to love God properly. God is the provider and sustainer of all things; therefore, if we allow Him to love through us, we will love like Him. We are told in the New Testament that we are to love our wives as Christ loves the church. We cannot properly lead our families and love our brides if we do not understand and relate to the love that Jesus has for His church.

Abraham and Sarah encountered difficult circumstances along the journey to possessing a godly marriage. They made mistakes, sinned against each other and God, and occasionally negatively impacted the lives of strangers. But God never gave up on them. Never. God blessed those who blessed them and cursed those who cursed them.

Family is important to God. Marriage was the first institution created by God. His reconciliation to a sinful world started with the family of Sarah and Abraham, and today Christians are adopted into the family of God. Now you see why Satan constantly works to destroy marriage, family, children, and lives. He will not stop and will resort to any tactic to get you off track. Don't ever think that a mistake you made is unforgivable to God, for His Son died for sins past, present, and future. Forgiveness, like grace, is both free and cannot be earned. Therefore, since you have been granted such a measure of forgiveness and grace, you must also respond to your spouse accordingly. Never give up on your marriage journey; God never will give up on you! Keep remembering it is a *journey* and not just a destination.

The last image I want to leave you with is the one of Abraham with a flickering torch held high. Abraham carried the fire—the torch—before he reached the summit of the rock where he was to sacrifice Isaac. This torch of fire can be a metaphor for us to illustrate how we must carry the fire of hope and faith on our marriage journey. Abraham never extinguished the fire. It was simply too hard to rekindle. Rubbing sticks together or using flint and steel worked, but it was slow, and the activity consumed too much time, so Abraham kept the fire burning. We therefore must carry God's torch of faith and hope in our marriage and protect its light.

You can become the Abraham or Sarah, the patriarch and matriarch, of your family, even if you do not come from a godly legacy. God wants to work in and through your life so that you, too, can be a blessing to generations of people. Your journey starts with the willingness and desire to follow God. It is all about you and your spouse becoming one flesh and staying focused on glorifying the One who made your marriage possible. Keep the fire burning, and enjoy the journey to a godly marriage!

Appendix

(Year) Plan

(This is to be completed individually and then combined to form a joint, annual family plan.)

Contribution List: (Initial contribution: 10% with the goal of growing annually).

Family Service/Spiritual:

Education/Involvement with (our child/children's) School:

Travel Plans (location and budget amount per month):

Fix-It List (cost):

Special Purchases/Planned (cost):

Career Plans/Goals:

Family Relationship with Spouse Focus:

Budgeting/Savings:

Debt List and Pay-off Goal/Schedule:

Exercise/Health Activity and Schedule:

Joint Five-Year Goals:

Prayer Focus:

Romantic Getaway/Activity:

About the Author

Lyndon (Lyn) Akins graduated from The University of Tennessee with a BS degree in Business Administration and holds a Master of Divinity Degree from Luther Rice University and Seminary. He is an ordained minister at Dunwoody Baptist Church, where he and his wife, Terry, teach young married couples and Lyn occasionally fills the pulpit for the senior pastor. Weekly podcasts and teaching notes from his material are available on www.ahigherplace. net, or podcasts may be downloaded from iTunes. Lyn currently travels the US for Aon Integramark as a Senior Vice President of Sales in the financial services market.

Lyn and Terry are originally from Maryville, TN, and they recently celebrated their 25th wedding anniversary. They are the parents of a teenage daughter, who is attending Marist High School in Atlanta. When the Akins are not camping, traveling, boating, or driving their 1930 Model A Ford, they enjoy quiet evenings at home with Georgia, their devoted yellow lab.

WinePressPublishing
Great Books, Defined.

To order additional copies of this book call:
1-877-421-READ (7323)
or please visit our website at
www.WinePressbooks.com

If you enjoyed this quality custom-published book,
drop by our website for more books and information.

www.winepresspublishing.com
"Your partner in custom publishing."

9 781414 120362